Make Your Calling and Election Sure

Christian Self-Improvement

Lucas Ward

Make Your Calling and Election Sure
© 2024 by DeWard Publishing Company
P.O. Box 290696, Tampa, FL 33687
www.deward.com

All rights reserved. No portion of this book may be reproduced in any form without written permission from the publisher.

Cover by Barry Wallace.

The preponderance of Bible quotations are taken from the The Holy Bible, English Standard Version®, copyright © 2001 by Crossway Bibles, a publishing ministry of Good News Publishers. Used by permission. All rights reserved." Any emphasis in Bible quotations is added.

Scriptures cited as ASV are from the 1901 American Standard Version. Where relevant, language has been updated to remove archaisms. Italics in ASV quotes are due to the translators' convention of italicizing words for which there is no direct reference in the original language.

Reasonable care has been taken to trace original sources for any excerpts and quotations appearing in this book and to document such information. For material not in the public domain, fair-use standards and practices were followed. Should any attribution be found to be incorrect or incomplete, the publisher welcomes written documentation supporting correction for subsequent printings.

Printed in the United States of America.

ISBN: 978-1-947929-33-3

For Roger Lindsey

who got me started

Contents

Preface and Acknowledgments. 7

Introduction 11

1. Faith. 17

2. A Living, Active Faith 21

3. In Your Faith Supply Virtue 32

4. In Your Virtue, Knoweldge 39

5. In Your Knowledge, Self-Control 46

6. In Your Self-Control, Patience. 52

7. In Your Patience, Godliness 57

8. In Your Godliness, Brotherly Kindness 63

9. In Your Brotherly Kindness, Love 70

10. Works of the Flesh vs. Fruit of the Spirit. 83

11. Joy 88

12. Peace 91

13. Kindness and Goodness 94

14. Faithfulness. 98

15. Meekness. 101

16. Wisdom 109

17. Humility 114

Conclusion. 118

Preface and Acknowledgments

When I took over the preaching duties at the Navarre church of Christ upon the retirement of Roger Lindsey, my modus operandi was primarily to think of all the things I needed to hear and to study out and preach those topics. I thought that if I needed these sermons, surely others would be helped as well. I have repeatedly said this from the pulpit to allay any charges of being judgmental. I am not judging when preaching; I am confessing. One of the things I need most is a warning against complacency. The Christian life should be one of continual growth and improvement as we better learn to be fruitful in the service of our Lord. It is too easy to feel that we are doing ok and fall into the rut of just attending "church" a few times a week and therefore begin to wither.

To combat this, one of the first large series of lessons I preached was on Christian self-improvement. We studied out the lists in 2 Peter and Galatians as well as a few of the times Jesus is said to have learned while He was on the earth. I tried to offer not just definitions and concepts but concrete methods of achieving growth in each of these areas. When the series was completed, it occurred to me that if each sermon was written out as a chapter, I would have a decent sized book when finished and my lessons may be able to help more people than just those who worship with me.

That is the purpose of this book. This is not academic or scholarly. You won't find much analysis of the Greek or discussions of odd liberal-agnostic views. This is meant to be a collection of practical lessons that can help everyday Christians live better, more fruitful lives for their Lord. If it can help just a few people in this way, then the book was worthwhile.

Fianlly, there are several people I would like to thank:

My parents, Keith and Dene Ward, taught me to think critically. They taught me to objectively analyze my ideas and discard theories that did not fit the facts, regardless of how treasured those theories might be. They taught me to be ruthless not only with my ideas, but with myself, always looking for the faults to improve upon, while rejoicing to stand in God's grace. More immediately, they were the first readers of this book and both corrected the poor writing and offered comments on the content.

My brother, Nathan Ward, who was willing to accept the manuscript as if from an author he didn't know and try to objectively determine whether it was worthy of being published. If he erred on the side of brotherly love, well, there is a first time for everything. As is usual in most DeWard publications, all the page layouts and final editing is his work. I don't know how he does it all. Brooke is an angel.

The Church in Navarre, which encouraged me as a neophyte and which allowed me to become the regular stand-in when Roger Lindsey was out of town. When Roger retired, the overwhelming majority of the church wanted me to take his place. They were patient and encouraging as I got my footing. In particular I want to mention Pat, who keeps me on my toes and keeps me in line, and John, who insists to everyone he meets that I am *so* much *better* than I used to be. I choose to take that as both a compliment and an impetus to continue to improve. Which, of course, is the whole point of this book.

Lucas Ward
July, 2024

Introduction

In the 1850s a little-known Swiss monk named Gregor Mendel began to experiment with pea plants. Over the next decade, through careful experimentation and note taking, Mendel invented the science of genetics. It would take a few more decades for the scientific community to embrace Mendel's discoveries and much was left to be learned, but Mendel is the one who kicked off genetic study. His discoveries aided our understanding of how traits are inherited, why selective breeding works, and where many diseases originate. Unfortunately, the study of genetics has also had an effect on social mores.

The American ethos which shaped the early centuries of our country from colonization to revolution and the founding of our republic to the conquering of the continent was self-determination and self-improvement. Almost everyone believed that anyone, given the opportunity, could intelligently choose his path in life and work to improve himself. In fact, one of our Presidents was illiterate until his wife taught him to read and then, while running a business and taking care of his family, he educated himself well enough to become President of the

United States. That ethos pervaded popular literature and drama at least as late as the early 1990s. A major theme of *Star Trek: The Next Generation* was the android Mr. Data continually striving to become more than merely the sum of his programming. Continually striving for self-improvement was part of the American way.

As our knowledge of genetics has increased, however, that ethos has died out. We have largely accepted the idea that our genes rule, and we have no choice in our lives. I remember when I was in High School in the mid-90s and scientists discovered that certain genes made some people more susceptible to alcoholism than others. Many of my friends said, "See, those people don't have a chance." I tried to point out that the genes merely made that person more susceptible, they didn't determine the outcome certainly. If the susceptible person never has the first drink, he won't become an alcoholic, I tried to say, but my friends denied that and declared that the genetics left no choice. That has largely become our society's viewpoint. Genetics are used as an excuse for everything. "This is how I'm programmed by my genes, and I can't possibly overcome that," most of America seems to say. Lt. Commander Data would be ashamed.

All kinds of behavior today are excused on the basis of genetics, from murder and all kinds of sexual perversions, to lying, outbursts of anger, alcohol/drug abuse, and even stealing. No one believes there is any point in trying to grow or change. What is most distressing, however, is that this belief has pervaded even the church. How often do we hear "Christians" say, "This is just how I am"? Any lesson in Bible class or sermon from the preacher exhorting improved behavior is met with "I know I lose my temper sometimes (or don't control my tongue, etc.) but that's just how I am. God made me this way, so He'll have to accept me." Maybe I'm just odd, but any statement declaring what God *has* to do seems immediately suspect.

In fact, "That's just how I am, I can't change" is not a Biblical concept at all. Just the opposite, the Bible teaches that God expects us to change: "Wash yourselves; make yourselves clean; remove the evil of your deeds from before my eyes; cease to do evil, learn to do good; seek justice, correct oppression; bring justice to the fatherless, plead the widow's cause" (Isa 1.16–17). How much plainer could it be? "Cease to do evil, learn to do good." We can learn to control ourselves and change, and God expects that: "For if you truly amend your ways and your deeds, if you truly execute justice one with another, if you do not oppress the sojourner, the fatherless, or the widow, or shed innocent blood in this place, and if you do not go after other gods to your own harm, then I will let you dwell in this place, in the land that I gave of old to your fathers forever" (Jer 7.5–7). Only if the Israelites amended their ways would God bless them. In other words, God expected then and today for us to change. We can, and must, overcome any built-in temptations we might have.

No one says that this is easy. It takes great effort. Paul tells Timothy to "Give diligence to present yourself approved unto God, a workman that needs not to be ashamed, handling aright the word of truth" (2 Tim

2.15 ASV). Diligence means continued, earnest effort. Diligence does not mean giving something one big hard try and then quitting. It is not a little bit of effort every now and then over a period of time. Diligence is ongoing and earnest effort, and this is the word Paul uses of the work Timothy (and we) needed to be approved of God. The Hebrews writer says the same thing about the effort needed to achieve the rest God has promised to His people (4.11). To be able to present ourselves as approved of God, or to be ready for the rest He promises, takes effort. Continuous, serious effort. It is not easy, but then things of value rarely come easily.

Not only does self-improvement require serious effort, it takes honest self-evaluation. This is perhaps the hardest thing to accomplish. After all, I can easily list what is wrong with everyone else in the church, but I'm perfect, right? My weaknesses, if I admit to any, are part of my charm and if I ever hurt anyone, either they had it coming or I apologize right away and who could expect more? Right? To turn my critical gaze upon myself as perceptively as I use it on others might be the most difficult thing God requires, but He does require it: "Try your own selves, whether you are in the faith; prove your own selves" (2 Cor 13.5 ASV). I must be regularly testing myself to ensure I am living as a Christian. In fact, James teaches that if we read the Bible without doing anything to improve ourselves, we are like fools who can't remember what they look like. Our regular Bible classes and sermons are not just for intellectual stimulation! We should leave knowing how to improve each week.

Ultimately, my salvation is my responsibility. Within the context of Christ's sacrifice and God's grace, no one is responsible for my eternal destination except me. This is what Peter teaches us: "Wherefore, brethren, give the more diligence to make your calling and election sure: for if you do these things, you shall never stumble" (2 Pet 1.10 ASV). Peter tells them, and by extension us, that it is up to them to make their election sure. They must give diligence so that their salvation is ensured and Peter says that if they follow his teaching on the subject, they won't stumble.

This book is intended as a study of the Bible's teaching about personal self-improvement. God doesn't just tell us to be better and then leave us guessing. He provides through His word several discussions and examples of personal improvement. We will examine those teachings together so that we can each make plans to continuously become more Christ-like.

If it is not yet clear, I am not writing this from a scholarly point of view. I don't have a string of degrees. I am an ordinary Christian who reads the Bible to learn to be better. The Bible was written to ordinary people who were expected to understand it and become disciples of Christ. I am writing this in the hopes that it will help ordinary people come to a better understanding of God's teaching on the area of personal improvement.

The most obvious place to start any discussion on Christian personal growth is in 2 Peter 1. In verse four, we see that God has granted us exceeding great promises that if we escape the corruption of lust in the world we may partake of the divine nature. (!) Talk about great promises! To be made like God, to share in what it means to be God, that is a goal beyond dreaming. Like most of what God is and does, this is so far past what anyone could conceive of that no one dared dream it and yet here is that promise. Therefore, Peter says, "for this very cause adding on your part all diligence, in your faith supply virtue; and in *your* virtue knowledge; and in *your* knowledge self-control; and in *your* self-control patience; and in *your* patience godliness; and in *your* godliness brotherly kindness; and in *your* brotherly kindness love" (2 Pet. 1:5-7 ASV). Here we find that diligence word again. The ESV reads "make every effort ..." Every effort. It will require disciplined, determined approach, but this building of ourselves will be worth it. Peter goes on to say that if we follow this improvement plan, we "will not be ineffective or unfruitful" and we will make our salvation sure. The first place to start is right at the beginning, with faith.

1

Faith

In Peter's self-improvement list, faith is presupposed: "in your faith, supply... ."[1] This makes the most basic kind of sense. If one doesn't have Christian faith, why would he bother to work on improving his Christian life? Faith is fundamental to walking with God: "And without faith it is impossible to please him, for whoever would draw near to God must believe that he exists and that he rewards those who seek him" (Heb 11.6).

Faith and belief are translated from the same Greek word, but both Biblically and otherwise faith involves much more than simple belief. It is a system of belief upon which one orders his life. Whether we are talking about ancient pagans, modern Muslims, or even atheists, their faith in something that cannot be absolutely proven informs their lives. Lately "science" has also taken its place as a faith that people hold. Not the scientific method—the concept of testing hypotheses and rejecting those that don't stand up to experimentation and then trying again—but the unquestioned belief that if some-

---

[1] Large parts of chapters 1 and 2 were adapted from Dene Ward's unpublished class book on faith with her permission.

one called a scientist said it, it must be absolutely true. If only Christians were as faithful to the Bible!

Christian faith begins, of course, with the belief in God's existence, but goes beyond that. After all, Abraham—the Father of the Faithful—spoke to God occasionally. He even served dinner to God (Gen 18). God's existence was not a matter of faith for Abraham—he knew God existed and yet his faith is lauded. His faith that was "reckoned to him for righteousness" (Gen 15.6 ASV) was faith that God would keep His promises. His faith in God's promises was so great that he offered the child of promise as a sacrifice when so ordered "accounting that God *is* able to raise up, even from the dead" (Heb 11.19 ASV) if necessary to keep His promises. Hebrews 11.6 again: Abraham believed not only in God's existence, but that God was a rewarder of those who seek Him. Moses, too, spoke to God, saw the backparts of His glory, and had no doubts as to the existence of God. Moses is also listed in Hebrews 11 for his faith in the promises that God had made. So, Biblical faith is not just faith in the existence of God, but trusting God to keep His promises. This is what we hold on to when all else is falling apart. When nothing is going as we expected and bad things keep piling up and we do not understand any of it, what we hold to is this faith in a God who always keeps His promises.

Our Faith's Foundation

So that raises the question, "On what is our faith founded?" God keeps His promises so we live our lives for Him, but how do I know what it means to live for Him? Or perhaps we first ask, "What are these great promises and how can I know them?"

Throughout history men have used many methods to try to discern what the gods wanted of them. They looked for various omens such as the flight formations of birds or astronomical events like eclipses. Sorcerers would read palms, the tea leaves, or cast animal bones. And, of course, the movement of the stars and planets were thought to hold much weight. Upon such things the pagans depended. In more modern times, religious peoples have depended on councils of wise men who decided what the doctrines of the church would be. Sometimes one great man would rise up to lead the people. One problem of this, of course, is that none of the councils agree. In the Catholic church alone dozens of councils have met amending the doctrines declared by the previous councils. Add the council of Episcopalian Bishops, the gatherings of Presbyters, and the Southern Baptist Association, among others, and we have hundreds of sincere, religious men all trying to tell us what we should believe and none of them agreeing. Is this how one's faith should be based?

The Biblical answer is so much simpler: "faith comes by hearing, and hearing by the word of Christ." (Rom 10.17 ASV). In other words, my faith isn't based on what other men teach me, but rather what Christ has taught me. So how do I know what Christ is teaching? It is pretty easy to figure out what Jesus was teaching in the Gospels, but what about the rest of the Bible? How do I know it is also the word of Christ? "The Holy Spirit, whom the Father will send in my name, will teach you all things and bring to your remembrance all that I have said to you" (John 14.26). This is what Jesus said to the Apostles on the night of the Last Supper. He promised that the Holy Spirit would help them remember all the Lord had taught them and would teach them the things that Jesus hadn't had time to teach, in His name. Therefore, when the Apostles wrote the New Testament, they were passing on the words of Christ (2 Pet 3.2). As to the Old Testament, Paul calls it a "tutor to bring us to Christ" (Gal 3.24) and also says it is able to make the man of God perfect (2 Tim 3.15–17). So, the Bible consists of the word of Christ and our faith is therefore based on the teachings of the Bible, and only on the teachings of the Bible. After all, one of the Lord's biggest rebukes against the Pharisees was that they taught "for doctrines the commandments of men" (Mark 7.7). They had elevated the teaching of their rabbis, specifically the oral traditions, above even the word of God. Isn't that exactly what we do when we are more interested in what the Pope (or the Southern Baptist association) says than in what the Bible teaches?

2

A Living, Active Faith

Again, faith as taught in the Bible is more than just belief. It is a system of belief that informs our lives. It is almost a living thing within us that can grow or shrivel up. Faith is discussed in the Bible as something that can increase, be strengthened, grow exceedingly, something upon which we can build ourselves (Luke 17.5; Acts 16.5; 2 Thess 1.3; Jude 20). Conversely, some have fallen away from the faith, been led astray from the faith, erred concerning the faith, abandoned the faith, and faith can also be denied (1 Tim 4.1; 6.10; 6.21; 5.12; Rev 2.13). If my faith can become so weak that I might abandon or deny it, or I might err in or be led astray from the faith, then I want to know what things might endanger my faith, so that I can be on guard.

One of the greatest of dangers is false teachers and false teaching. My faith must be built on the word of Christ, but sometimes what we think is Gospel is, instead, error. This can lead to faith being overthrown (2 Tim 2.18). Sometimes the false teaching sounds so good or so right that few notice the difference. In 1 Timothy 4.1 Paul calls false teaching "the doctrine of demons" but acknowledges that such is often "seducing." It sounds good. Often we wish it were true. Therefore, we are easily swayed to that false doctrine. This is why it is so important to follow the example of the noble Bereans, who were "examining the Scriptures daily, whether these things [the teachings of Paul] were so" (ASV). If they wanted to backstop the teaching of an miracle worker with Scripture, how much care should I take with what my uninspired local preacher teaches? (Including the one writing this book!)

Another danger to my faith is a love of money and material things. Everyone knows that Paul says in 1 Timothy 6.10 that "the love of money is a root of all kinds of evil" (ASV) because those who chase money often are willing to do horrible things to get it. That goes hand in hand with Jesus' teaching in Matthew 6 that man cannot serve both God and Mammon. If my life is devoted to building wealth, then am I storing any treasure in Heaven? A final thought on the dangers of materialism—even the righteous man whose focus is on God can be swayed by riches if he loses his focus. "The name of Jehovah is a strong tower; The righteous runs into it, and is safe. The rich man's wealth is his strong city, And as a high wall in his own imagination" (Prov 18:10-11 ASV). The rich man, if he isn't careful, can come to rely on his wealth as protector, rather than God. Before we scoff at this, how often do we hear someone say something like, "I know I'm going to be okay for retirement because I saved and invested!" Where is this person's faith? In God, or in his 401k?

A final thing to be wary of is the combination platter of our passions and our idle time. In 1 Timothy 5.11–12,

A Living, Active Faith | 23

Paul explains that the reason he teaches younger widows to remarry rather than being enrolled in the church's daily ministration is because their passions will lead them to sin and the idle time could turn them into gossips and busybodies. He was concerned that their faith could not stand up to that one-two punch. This should be a concern for us as well. We live in a society that worships passion and our nation is the wealthiest and most technologically advanced in history, giving the average person incredible amounts of free time. Do we use that free time as true servants of God should, or do we while away the hours playing video games, watching our favorite streaming services and generally goofing-off? Do we rein in our passions, or have our appetites truly become our god? (Phil 3.19). The danger to our faith here is not so much that we will err in our faith or abandon it, but rather that it will die on the vine. We become so caught up in amusing ourselves, after only a 40-hour work week, that we never feed our faith. We never exercise ourselves toward godliness, and our faith shrivels.

On the other hand, faith can be built up—a good thing since the premise of this book is personal growth! The Apostles had the right idea in Luke 17. When faced with a task that took more faith than they believed they possessed, they asked the Lord for an increase (v 5). Prayer to God for help in our efforts to grow is the best way to begin the endeavor and is essential as we move forward. Prayer not only calls upon the benevolent power of God as a help, it keeps us focused on our goals and maintains our impetus.

Also, as dangerous as false teaching can be to our faith, good gospel preaching is equally good for growing our faith. In 1 Corinthians 2.4–5, Paul says he preached so that their faith would stand. In Colossians 1.23 he says that their faith must not move away from the hope of the gospel, *which they had heard preached*. It seems beyond obvious that repeated hearings of that gospel would aid in keeping their faith steadfast. This fits right in with Ephesians 4.23 and Romans 12.2, which both remind us that as Christians, we must constantly renew ourselves. Putting the old man of sin to death and living our new faith is a continual effort.

Finally, Colossians 2.7 nearly equates being established in the faith with abounding in thanksgiving. This makes the hardest kind of sense. At base, our faith is in God keeping His promises. God's promises are based on the sacrifice and subsequent resurrection of His Son. We cannot remember that sacrifice without being thankful, and giving thanks for the sacrifice renews our faith in the promises built upon that sacrifice.

An Active Faith

When we discuss the need for our faith to be an active one, we almost always reference James 2. The point is made most clearly, even bluntly here: "Show me your faith apart from your works and I will show you my faith by my works," and, "Faith apart from works is dead" (vv 18, 26) It doesn't get much plainer than that. However, one might get the idea that this is the only passage in the Bible that teaches this principle. Was James a crank with weird ideas that somehow got his writings included in the New Testament? No, in fact passages similar to James 2 pervade the New Testament. In Acts 6.7 they were "obedient to the faith." We are to" walk by faith" (2 Cor 5.7). Faith should be " working through love" (Gal 5.6), and we are to be "striving for the faith" (Phil 1.27). In Philippians 2.17, faith is described as "sacrifice and service" and 2 Thessalonians 1.11 discusses "every work of faith," while Titus 3.15 speaks of those who "love us in faith." New Testament teaching so abounds in works of faith and faith working and us striving for and being obedient to the faith that one wonders how anyone who had given it even a cursory reading could come up with the notion of "faith only."

"Ok," someone might say, "so our faith should lead us to work. Maybe it is a onetime event and then I spend the rest of my life merely maintaining my belief?" As many times as we hear "just pray the sinner's prayer and then you'll be fine," one can understand how a person might believe in the one-time work of faith. "I'll just write a check to Oral Roberts University and then I'll be fine," or "I'll just be baptized and then, other than taking the Lord's Supper every Sunday, I'll just maintain my belief and I'll be fine." This is not what the Bible teaches. The Christian life is often referred to as a walk, e.g., "we walk by faith" (2 Cor 5.7). That strongly implies that faith remains active throughout our lives. In Ephesians 4:17 and following, Paul discusses the on-going change of life Christianity brings, the contrast between the old life and the new. In Philippians 1:27, faith is called our "manner of life" and faith is a calling in 2 Thessalonians 1.11. Have you ever spoken to someone who thought that being a teacher was their calling? Or being a nurse or detective, etc.? Do they ever stop working at those things? No, that calling defines them. Our faith is our calling. It is how we define ourselves, who we are, and how we live our lives. Faith cannot be just a one-time thing.

In the New Testament we find a few examples of people who did believe, but did not act upon their belief. They gave a mental assent to the truth, but would not live their faith. Let's see how the Bible deals with them.

"And there was much murmuring among the multitudes concerning him: some said, He is a good man; others said, Not so, but he leads the multitude astray. Yet no man spoke openly of him for fear of the Jews" (John 7.12–13 ASV). Here we have some of the people who believed in Jesus, but for fear of the Jewish leaders would not speak out for Him. Another case is John 12.42–43: "Nevertheless even of the rulers many believed on him; but because of the Pharisees they did not confess *it*, lest they should be put out of the synagogue: for they loved the glory *that is* of men more than the glory *that is* of God" (ASV). While the first example may be seen as ambivalent, this passage clearly denounces these men who loved man's glory more than God's. This is not a pretty portrayal.

An active faith not only defines us, it should change who we are. Look at how much Paul changed because of his faith: "They only were hearing it said, 'He who used to persecute us is now preaching the faith he once tried to destroy'" (Gal 1.23). Paul went from being the most rabid persecutor of the church at that time—one who broke

A Living, Active Faith | 27

into homes in order to drag people off to prison, who voted for their execution and who was willing to march nearly 200 miles for the chance to arrest some more—to being a preacher of that same faith.

That, itself, is an astounding change, but having an active faith is about more than just obeying a few new rules while leading essentially the same life we always led before. We see that clearly in the life of Paul. He didn't just stop persecuting the church and start preaching the Gospel (if one can say "just" about such a sea-change) while remaining essentially the same person. Paul's faith changed everything about who he was. Look at how he describes himself pre-faith: "circumcised on the eighth day, of the people of Israel, of the tribe of Benjamin, a Hebrew of Hebrews; as to the law, a Pharisee; as to zeal, a persecutor of the church; as to righteousness under the law, blameless" (Phil 3.5–6). A blameless Hebrew of Hebrews and a Pharisee to boot.

If I were going to describe the Pharisees by two traits it would be these. First, they were extremely careful to obey the law, to the point of inventing rules around the law intended to keep them far from any chance of rule-breaking. Second, they were extremely proud of how they kept the law. Remember the parable of the two men praying. The Pharisee stood up and thanked God that he was not like other men, that he didn't commit these sins but he did do all these righteous things and he wasn't even weak like the poor tax collector next to him (Luke 18.9–14). That pride defined who the Pharisees were, and Paul was one. While I'd like to think that Paul wouldn't have been one of the hypocritical Pharisees who argued so much with the Lord, that is the religious party to which he was affiliated and, pre-Christ, he was proud of that affiliation.

Now look at how much Paul had changed: "To the Jews I became as a Jew, in order to win Jews. To those under the law I became as one under the law (though not being myself under the law) that I might win those under the law. To those outside the law I became as one outside the law (not being outside the law of God but under the law of Christ) that I might win those outside the law. To the weak I became weak, that I might win the weak. I have become all things to all people, that by all means I might save some" (1 Cor 9.20–22). This is how Paul describes his efforts at evangelism, but can you imagine one of the Pharisees of the Gospels acting as if he were without the Law in order to win those outside the Law? No! Obeying the Law defined who he was. He would never pretend to be outside the Law! Better to let someone die in his ignorance than to pretend to be out of the Law. Or can you ever imagine one of those Pharisees pretending to be weak to reach the weak? No! They were proud of their religious strength and despised the weak. Paul's faith not only changed the way he worshiped God, it altered his very personality. At a very fundamental level it changed who he was. If our faith isn't acting on our hearts to change who we are, then maybe our faith isn't as active as it should be.

This active faith can be a bit too aggressive sometimes, though, either through ignorance or zeal (or both). We see this in the story of Peter lopping off the ear of Malchus in the Garden of Gethsemane. Peter knew that Jesus was the Messiah to come and he was willing to face a cohort of soldiers on his own to buy with his death the time Jesus needed to escape arrest. Peter did not understand the spiritual nature of Jesus' kingdom nor the plan of salvation God had enacted which depended on Jesus' sacrifice. He was overly aggressive in his faith due to a lack of understanding of God's plans. In Luke 9.52–55 we read the story of the Samaritan village which would not allow Jesus to stay there because he was on his way to Jerusalem. James and John, offended for Jesus, asked "Lord, do you want us to tell fire to come down from heaven and consume them?" (v 54). These people had, after all, refused the Son of God. They had insulted deity. They deserved death! And yet, Jesus rebuked James and John for their overly-zealous faith.

We, too, can sometimes become overly aggressive in our faith. Taking the Lord's Name in vain is blasphemy and an insult to God, but if we were going around slapping in the mouth all who we heard doing so (like Indiana Jones's father did to him) we wouldn't accomplish much more than receiving a few assault charges. More realistically, we are often too aggressive in our faith in how we speak to each other. True, Jesus was often blunt to the point of rudeness when He spoke to people, and we are commanded to be imitators of Christ, but Jesus was also kind, patient and soft spoken when that was called for. So, we cannot just claim to be following Christ's pattern whenever we blast someone to cinders when we address them. We are also taught to "speak the truth *in love*" (Eph 4.13) and to "let your words always be with grace, seasoned with salt" (Col 4.6). Why do we put salt on food? Because it makes things taste better, right? So, we season our words with salt when we take the time to think of how to say a needed thing in such a way that it "tastes" as good as possible to the hearer. In all of this we remember that "the wisdom that is from above is *first* pure *then* peaceable" (Jas 3.17).

How do we temper our active faith so that the activity doesn't morph into unchecked aggression? First, note that in 1 Timothy 6.11 the man of God is to "pursue righteousness, godliness, faith, love, patience and meekness." Look at the things we are to pursue along with our faith. Make special note of three of these. Godliness and meekness both have to do with keeping our focus on God, always thinking of what He would want, rather than what we would want, and always being far more concerned with Him receiving glory than receiving any glory ourselves. If we are living those attributes and add love to the mixture then we will, as a matter of course, always work to say the right things in the right way. We will show patience and long-suffering. Secondly, remember what Peter says regarding how we should gird ourselves, "All of you gird yourselves with humility, to serve one another" (1 Pet 5.5 ASV). If I am putting on humility with my clothes each morning it is unlikely that I will have a self-righteous attitude that leads me to treat others with holier-than-thou disdain.

Isn't it ironic that Peter, the first of our examples of overly aggressive faith due to, in his case, a lack of under-

A Living, Active Faith | 31

standing, is the apostle who wrote the most often used list of personal growth goals in the Bible? It is Peter who said, "for this very cause adding on your part all diligence, in your faith supply virtue; and in *your* virtue knowledge; and in *your* knowledge self-control; and in *your* self-control patience; and in *your* patience godliness; and in *your* godliness brotherly kindness; and in *your* brotherly kindness love" (2 Pet 1.5–7)

It starts with our belief that Jesus is the Christ, the Son of God, and then we grow that faith and our full Christian personalities upon that faith. That is the journey we now begin.

3

In Your Faith Supply Virtue

I am not a linguist at all and rely on the scholars for word meanings but, as I understand it, virtue just means excellence and could be applied to any endeavor. Technically, one could therefore call Willie Mays a virtuous baseball player. After all, he was a career .300 hitter with 660 home runs and was one of the best defenders to ever play in center field. That's pretty excellent. Of course, in the Bible virtue refers to excellence of character. A virtuous person does the right thing even when no one is watching. This is the person who does the right thing whether or not they receive any benefit from it. In an interview shortly after he won the role, the actor Chris Evans described Captain America as the kind of man he wishes he himself was, who did the right thing because it was right. That concept is what virtue is all about. While we can use this terminology of "good" non-Christians, from Christians even more is expected.

First, let's take note of the fact that virtue is a characteristic of God: "But you are a chosen race, a royal priesthood, a holy nation, a people for his own possession, that you may proclaim the excellencies of him who

In Your Faith Supply Virtue | 33

called you out of darkness into his marvelous light" (1 Pet 2.9). The word "excellencies" in this passage is the same Greek word as "virtue" in 2 Peter 1.5. Of course, "him who called you out of darkness and into his marvelous light" refers to God and it is His excellencies, or virtues, that we are proclaiming. We see this word being used of God's character again in 2 Peter 1.3: "seeing that his divine power has granted unto us all things that pertain to life and godliness through the knowledge of him who called by his own glory and virtue" (ASV) When we think about our righteous, holy God who is light and love, who cannot lie and who Jesus said was the only one who is good, and we see that His character is said to be excellent or virtuous, that in itself helps us to better understand the concept of virtue.

When I am trying to wrap my head around a Biblical concept, I often turn to the wisdom literature. The nature of the Hebrew poetry in the Psalms (parallelism, in which a concept is repeated in different ways) offers built-in definitions and the Proverbs offer pithy discussions on a wide variety of subjects. The word virtue is not used in the Old Testament, but two closely related terms are: righteousness and integrity. If virtue is doing the right thing because it is the right thing whether or not anyone will notice or reward, then obviously the person who does that has a certain integrity in his beliefs. Righteousness is closely related, but different from virtue—virtue being excellence of character and righteousness being a legal term meaning to do the right thing according to the law. Of course, a virtuous person would naturally do the right thing according to the law. So in both cases there are similarities. There may therefore be some benefit to our study of virtue in a short look at what we can learn about righteousness/integrity from the wisdom literature.

In Psalm 31.17–18, David identifies himself as the righteous man who is being persecuted by the evil. He claims as his salvation that he called upon the Lord. This isn't a person just interested in checking off the rules of the Law. This is a person who has and wants to maintain a relationship with God, who feels free to call upon Him and who is righteous. Similarly, in Psalm 64.10: "Let the righteous one rejoice in the LORD and take refuge in him! Let all the upright in heart exult!" In this verse it is clear that righteousness is not a soulless, emotionless enterprise. The righteous rejoice and exult in the Lord. This is not a checkoff following of Moses' Law, but a man whose obedience founds a relationship with God that thrills him. This rejoicing in the following of God's law surely shows the character of the righteous man. An excellent character. This attitude of joy is also seen in Psalm 68.3: "But let the righteous be glad; let them exult before God: Yea, let them rejoice with gladness." Also in Psalm 7.8, "… judge me, O LORD, according to my righteousness and according to the integrity that is in me." And Psalm 25.21: "May integrity and uprightness preserve me, for I wait for you." These two passages link integrity and righteousness, as if the person who is righteous is so because of who he is inside. This person relies on God's character. In Psalm 7 he wants to be judged for his righteousness and integrity. He knows implicitly that God is a righteous judge. In Psalm 25 he says he is waiting for God. Nothing can deter him from God and he believes that God will maintain the relationship between them. In all these passages we see excellence of character (virtue) at work and that virtue is based upon the relationship the virtuous person has with God. He calls upon the Lord, rejoices in the Lord, wants to be judged by the Lord and waits for the Lord. That close, dependent relationship with God is where virtue can lead us.

So, how do I work on increasing my virtue? After all, this is a fundamental change of character, not just controlling myself regarding one or two issues. This isn't just refusing to participate in coarse jesting, this is reaching a point where we do not even understand the dirty jokes people tell us because we never think about such things. This is becoming the person who is disgusted by the temptations around him, rather than the one who must exert intense self-control to overcome them. This is becoming the person who does the right thing because it is the right thing. How do I accomplish that?

Consider the relationship between virtue and righteousness. If the virtuous person naturally does righteousness because of who he is, then practicing righteousness daily will ingrain a habit leading us to become righteous by second nature. So, we need to learn what it is that God demands of us and strive to do those things. The Psalmist says, "Your testimonies are righteous forever; give me understanding and I shall live," and, "I have sworn and confirmed it, that I will observe thy righteous ordinances" (Ps 119.144, 106 ASV), and John adds, "For this is the love of God, that we keep His commandments" (1 John 5.3). Again, working to learn and follow His law consistently will instill new habits which is the first step to growing our virtue.

Embedding those right ways deeper into ourselves entails engaging our minds as well: "Blessed is the man who walks not in the counsel of the wicked, nor stands in the way of sinners, nor sits in the seat of scoffers; but his delight is in the law of the LORD, and on his law he meditates day and night" (Ps 1.1–2). The blessed man in this passage delights in and meditates on God's word. Meditation in the Bible is a different animal from the emptying of the mind and centering of oneself that is taught in Eastern mysticism. Biblical meditation is deep thought upon a subject. Musing upon that subject from every angle and trying to come to a complete understanding of the subject. The importance of meditation on God's word is repeatedly mentioned throughout the Psalms (e.g., 63.6; 77.12; 119.15, 27, 48; etc.). If what I routinely think about largely determines who I am, and if I want to change my basic character to one that is more virtuous, then I must change my thinking. There was a concept in the computer industry back in the 1980s and '90s called GIGO—Garbage In, Garbage Out—meaning computers cannot improve upon their inputs. They are only as accurate as the data one enters. If one enters false data, one receives false answers. This is also true of a person's character. If all I ever think about is college football, Marvel movies, and pretty girls, then what are the odds that I'll be of a virtuous character instead of a shallow, vulgar character? This is why Paul wrote, "Finally, brethren, whatsoever things are true, whatsoever things are honorable, whatsoever things are just, whatsoever things are pure, whatsoever things are lovely, whatsoever things are of good report; if there be any virtue, and if there be any praise, think on these things." (Phil 4.8 ASV).

My maternal grandfather, Gerald Ayers ("Papa"), is a prime example. In my teens my brother and I would often help Papa around his property or watch him tinker with things in his garage or shop. At some point I became aware that whenever we were working together, Papa was almost always humming or whistling or singing hymns under his breath. I also noticed that the large collection of cassette tapes he owned were nearly all collections of hymns sung acapella by professional choruses or amateur church groups. I also realized about the same time that I had never, ever witnessed Papa lose his temper. I had on rare occasions seen him angry, but he never lost his temper. Do you think that maybe the fact that his mind was constantly "on the things that are above" helped him achieve and maintain that excellence of character? I do.

Like the blessed man in Psalm 1, to improve our characters we must not only meditate on Him and His word, but we need to remove ourselves from the scoffers. If we surround ourselves with friends who speak vulgarly, who joke coarsely, and who speak constantly of their conquests, what is likely to be on our minds? The TV programs today are all humanistic, hedonistic, or both. If I spend hours daily watching those shows and 15 minutes daily in God's word, what is likely to happen to my character? As Paul said, "Bad company ruins good morals" (1 Cor 15.33).

To work to improve our virtue and become a person of excellent character is not an easy or short task. It means overcoming bad habits and bad character traits. It means replacing those traits with better traits. It means changing how we think and what we think about. It is not easy, but it can be done and it is a worthwhile effort. "You may become partakers of the divine nature ... For in this way there will be richly provided for you an entrance into the eternal kingdom of our Lord and Savior Jesus Christ" (2 Pet 1.4, 11).

4

In Your Virtue, Knowledge

We are to grow in knowledge. Knowledge of what, exactly? Somehow, I don't think memorizing Mickey Mantle's statistics year-by-year is what Paul had in mind. Nor is a comprehensive knowledge of Baroque music nor Constitutional law. So, what? The law of God, right? The doctrine that we must live by, this we must know. After all,

> The law of the LORD is perfect, reviving the soul; the testimony of the LORD is sure, making wise the simple; the precepts of the LORD are right, rejoicing the heart; the commandment of the LORD is pure, enlightening the eyes; the fear of the LORD is clean, enduring forever; the rules of the LORD are true, and righteous altogether." (Ps 19.7–9)

Paul also acknowledges the importance of knowing the doctrine and will of God: "we have not ceased to pray for you, asking that you may be filled with the knowledge of his will in all spiritual wisdom and understanding, so as to walk in a manner worthy of the Lord, fully pleasing to him: bearing fruit in every good work and increasing in the knowledge of God" (Col 1.9–10) If we do not know what His commandments are, we cannot follow them. If we do not know His will for our lives, we cannot fulfill that will. So, knowing the sound doctrine is exceedingly important, but that is just the beginning of knowledge: "Teach me good judgment and knowledge, for I believe in your commandments" (Ps 119.66). The psalmist already believes in, and therefore knows, God's commandments and he understands that good judgment and knowledge proceeds from that basic level.

Peter and Paul agree that a deep knowledge of God Himself should be the goal of all Christians. Peter tells us "His divine power has granted to us all things that pertain to life and godliness, through the knowledge of him who called us to his own glory and excellence" (2 Pet 1.3). In other words, the means by which God grants us all things is the knowledge of Him. Paul prays for the Ephesian church to grow in the knowledge of Him (Eph 1.17) and tells the Philippians that the knowledge of Christ is worth sacrificing everything (Phil 3:8). After all, "the knowledge of the Holy One is insight" (Prov 9.10). If you wish to gain more insight, get to know your savior a bit better.

Growth in knowledge is more than just a goal shared by Christians, it is an expectation of God's for all Christians. In 2 Corinthians 8.7 Paul, in exhorting the Corinthians to grow in another area, lists several things they would all be growing in. Knowledge is one of those categories. Paul presupposes that they are working to grow in knowledge because it is an obvious requisite. And we cannot discuss growth in knowledge without turning to Hebrews 5.12–6.2:

> For though by this time you ought to be teachers, you need someone to teach you again the basic principles of the or-

In Your Virtue, Knowledge | 41

acles of God. You need milk, not solid food, for everyone who lives on milk is unskilled in the word of righteousness, since he is a child. But solid food is for the mature, for those who have their powers of discernment trained by constant practice to distinguish good from evil. Therefore let us leave the elementary doctrine of Christ and go on to maturity, not laying again a foundation of repentance from dead works and of faith toward God, and of instruction about washings, the laying on of hands, the resurrection of the dead, and eternal judgment.

At least three points are relevant to our discussion. First, the Hebrew writer had expected these Christians to have grown by this point. They should have been teachers. Yes, James 3.1 says that not everyone should lead group studies or preach the Gospel, but every Christian should be able to tell their friends and neighbors about the Gospel and to give a reason for the hope they have (1 Pet 3.15). Even if we are not able to lead classes, our personal knowledge should be continually growing. We should be able to participate in ever more serious discussions of Biblical topics. Instead of being ready to teach, these brethren had regressed. "you need someone to teach you again." And so our second point, a warning that if we aren't working to grow in our knowledge of Him and His word we are going backwards. Like many things, if you don't use it, you lose it.

Finally, notice in the first two verses of chapter six that there are deeper, richer thoughts in Biblical knowledge than just the five steps of salvation and the five acts of worship. My father is one of the best Bible students I know of. Not a scholar in the sense of advanced degrees, but a student who has spent the last 50 years reading and studying, thinking about and meditating on the Bible. With all that wealth of knowledge built up, he delights in little more than getting together with two or three friends, all of whom are near-equals as Bible students, and discovering some new bit of Bible knowledge he hadn't known before, some new viewpoint from which to understand a passage or a linkage between passages that had been overlooked. No matter how much we learn, we can never exhaust the potentials of God's word. We don't need special qualifications to learn. My Dad likes to tell the story of some mind-blowing bit of knowledge he had just discovered which he ran off to tell his father—whose highest education level was the eleventh grade. Granddad listened carefully to what Dad was saying and then replied, "Yep, your uncle Carl and I were just talking about that while we were fixing the fence last week." It doesn't take fancy degrees or qualifications to know God's word; it just takes determination. "I will meditate on your precepts and fix my eyes on your ways" (Ps 119.15).

Since growth in our knowledge of Him and His word is expected of His people, it should not come as a surprise that there are consequences for a lack of knowledge. The Old Testament prophets attributed the destruction of the ten northern tribes to a lack of knowledge: "Therefore my people go into exile for lack of knowledge" (Isa 5.13). And, "Hear the word of the LORD, O children of Israel, for the LORD has a controversy with the inhabitants of the land. There is no faithfulness or steadfast love, and no knowledge of God in the land. ... My people are destroyed for lack of knowledge; because you have rejected knowledge, I reject you" (Hos 4.1, 6). This problem continued in the New Testament era as well. In discussing the first century Jews who refused Christianity, Paul wrote, "For I bear them witness that they have a zeal for God, but not according to knowledge. For, being ignorant of the righteousness of God, and seeking to establish their own, they did not submit to God's righteousness" (Rom 10.2–3). Paul describes a people zealous for God and for righteousness but who didn't have the proper knowledge. In trying to find their own way to God, they forgot to humble themselves to God's will. While Paul was speaking of people of his own time, his remarks ring true of the larger "Christian" world today. "You don't need to be baptized, just pray the sinner's prayer." "You can choose the church of your choice." And on and on. None of those statements match the doctrine in the Bible, but many zealous people are fooled by them because of a lack of knowledge. I don't know many things sadder than that. Many of these people are sincere in their desire to serve God, but their lack of knowledge will lead to destruction, just like the ancient Israelites.

How do we grow in our knowledge of God and of God's word? There is no magic pill. It takes work: "Give diligence to present yourself approved unto God, a workman that needs not to be ashamed, handling aright the word of truth" (2 Tim. 2:15 ASV). To give diligence is to give consistent, earnest effort. In teaching a High School Bible class about Bible study, my father once said that while he loved to study God's word, and those moments of insight when he came to a deeper understanding of truth were delightful indeed, there were also times when the work required to achieve those insights was just plain drudgery. For example, in preparing this chapter, I at least skimmed every passage in the Bible that had the word knowledge in it. Let me tell you, those were two very boring hours! But the benefit outweighs the boredom and often it is far from boring.

To continue our knowledge growth beyond the superficial we must do more than just have our Bible class studies ready each week. We must go beyond simple daily Bible readings. In 2 Timothy 3.14–15 Paul tells Timothy to abide in the sacred writings. Timothy's existence should be in the scriptures. This is a concept well known to the ancient psalmist: "Oh how love I your law! It is my meditation all the day" (Ps 119.97). We spend our days thinking about our daily readings. We ponder over how what we read today connects with what we read yesterday and last week. We consider alternate viewpoints. We live in the word.

Doing this well takes a bit more effort than merely reading. We need to understand that verses are not individual units of thought, that the Bible is written in sentences and paragraphs like any normal discussion of ideas. To grasp the concepts discussed, we need to attempt to outline the thoughts being put forward. Notice repeated words or phrases. Are the ideas in consecutive paragraphs connected and progressing to a conclusion? We need to be aware of words that connect concepts together like "therefore." To really get into the grunt work of Bible Study, one can begin word studies, in which one reads all the passages in which a word is used and what can be learned about that word from the context in which it is used. It is amazing how much deeper an understanding of Biblical concepts can be achieved in this way. It does, however, take diligence.

Finally, our knowledge of God, Himself, can be improved by a study of His actions, including creation itself. Paul makes it clear in Romans 1.19–20 that God felt He had left enough clues in creation to keep the pagans from idolatry. Again, the psalmists: "I will ponder all your work, and meditate on your mighty deeds" (Ps 77.12); "When I remember you upon my bed, and meditate on you in the watches of the night…" (Ps 63.6). We can learn a lot about God by thinking about what He does. We can learn of God's sense of humor by looking at the giraffe and the platypus. We can see His love of beauty for beauty's sake in the sunsets each evening. We can see His wisdom and extreme understanding in the workings of the creation around us, whose laws we can barely grasp. All of these things which we can learn from observing His works should lead us to the thought, "I want to get to know this God better." And that should lead us right back to a study of His word.

5

In Your Knowledge, Self-Control

As we study self-control, we quickly come to understand its central place in the Christian life. Paul lists self-control as part of the fruit of the Spirit (Gal 5.22–23). Contrast that with the description of the wicked society in 2 Timothy 3.2–4: "For men shall be lovers of self, lovers of money, boastful, haughty, railers, disobedient to parents, unthankful, unholy, without natural affection, implacable, slanderers, without self-control, fierce, no lovers of good, traitors, headstrong, puffed up, lovers of pleasure rather than lovers of God" (ASV). Notice that these wicked people not only have no self-control, they are described as lovers of pleasure rather than God which seems almost a definition for a lack of self-control. Their desires rule them, rather than ruling their desires. Paul mentions them also in Romans: "Now I beseech you, brethren, mark them that are causing the divisions and occasions of stumbling, contrary to the doctrine which you learned: and turn away from them. For they that are such serve not our Lord Christ, but their own belly" (16.17–18 ASV). Serving their belly rather than Christ means allowing their appetites to rule them. When thinking of appetites like this, don't just think of eating or drinking or other fleshly desires like sexual immorality. In the above passage the ones who are serving their bellies are causing divisions in the church. Here the appetites are apparently for power, acknowledgment, or just juicy gossip. Their lack of control in those areas is ripping apart the people of God. This shows the importance of self-control in the lives of Christians.

Self-control requires walking in a new life in Christ (Rom 6). We were baptized into His death (v 3) that the body of sin may be put away and we should no longer be enslaved to sin (v 6). Because of this we are, like Christ, now dead to sin but alive to God (vv 10-11). Paul's conclusion: "Let not sin therefore reign in your mortal body, that you should obey the lusts thereof: neither present your members unto sin *as* instruments of unrighteousness; but present yourselves unto God, as alive from the dead, and your members *as* instruments of righteousness unto God. For sin shall not have dominion over you, for you are not under law but under grace." (vv 12–14 ASV). In our new lives with Christ we choose not to allow sin to rule us—we rule it as we serve God rather than our sinful appetites. This is rarely achieved in completeness, but God has called us to strive towards this goal. "My little children, I write this unto you that you may not sin," John tells us (1 John 2.1 ASV). This is the walk laid before us and we must always strive to walk the walk, rather than just talking the talk as happens all too often in churches. This walk obviously requires self-control as we no longer allow ourselves to follow every whim of mind or hormonal surge of body and instead "look unto things above" and follow God's direction. Perfection in this life will not be achieved, even John admits this as he ends that verse with, "and if any man sin we have an advocate with the Father, Jesus Christ the righteous," but we must stop using this as an excuse to continually give in to our urges and acknowledge what it really is: an abject failure that makes us abysmally disgusting in the eyes of the Lord. "You are slaves of the one whom you obey" (Rom 6.16). Self-control is your choice.

While perfection in this area may not be expected, growth in our ability to rule ourselves is expected. "For you are still of the flesh…" (1 Cor 3.3 ASV). Paul was upset to learn that the members of the Corinthian church were still following the urges of the flesh, behaving after the manner of men rather than according to the teaching of God. In the preceding verses Paul was not upset that they were still fleshly or carnal when they had just been converted to Christianity. They were babes in Christ! However, he had expected them to grow in self-control and spirituality by this point in their Christian walk and he was upset and disappointed to find them as they were. Clearly, Christians are expected to grow in the area of self-control.

How? Well, to steal from Nike's slogan, "Just do it." I am not being flippant; the more one does anything, the easier it becomes to do that thing. For example, when I first started riding my bicycle, nine miles almost did me in. Now that I've built myself up to riding 13.5

miles regularly, if I do a mere nine mile ride I feel as if I am just getting started when the ride is over. Using exercise as an example is not an accident. Again, look at Paul's analogy, "Every athlete exercises self-control in all things. They do it to receive a perishable wreath, but we an imperishable" (1 Cor 9.25). Just like physical exercise, it takes effort, but the more I tell myself "no" and make it stick, the easier I can control myself in that area. The temptations never go away completely, but handling them becomes more and more a habitual thing.

Another way to stay in control is to remove myself from as many temptations as possible. When people are in financial trouble, what do they often do as they begin to budget? They cut up their credit cards so they won't be able to use them. Alcoholics generally stay out of bars. In like manner, one should avoid the things that tempt him as best as he can. This might be called self-control by proxy, but it works. If "looking to lust" is a problem, perhaps one should stay off the public beaches where the pretty young things put themselves on display. If one has a tendency to gossip with certain people who encourage that behavior, then perhaps he should limit his time with those friends. 1 Corinthians 10.13 does say that God will always provide a way of escape for temptations, but a person should stop jumping into the fire and then praying for God to show up with an extinguisher! The temptations that naturally occur in life are tough enough to defeat, we certainly don't need to be courting the danger.

Self-control often boils down to just hanging on. Don't quit, don't let go, keep hanging on: "I hold fast my righteousness and will not let it go; my heart does not reproach me for any of my days" (Job 27.6). This was Job's outlook. He was going to hold on and not let go. Was he tempted to leave his righteousness behind? Sure, even his wife told him he should just give up (2.9), but Job was determined to hold on. My father is a retired probation officer and he dealt with drug addicts and drug counselors as a matter of course. Often the best drug counselors are recovering addicts themselves. Dad told the story of one of the best counselors he knew who was a recovering cocaine addict. He had been clean for 20 years and still sometimes had almost overwhelming urges for a fix. He told Dad that sometimes he would just sit at his desk and hang on to the desk because he knew if he let go, he'd get up and go buy some cocaine, but if he kept ahold of the desk he wouldn't be able to go. So, he sat there and just hung on until the urge passed. If he can do that for his drug addiction, why can't I do that in regards to my various sin addictions? If I become angry and know that opening my mouth will release a vile spewing of wrathful comments, maybe I should clench my jaws until the urge passes. If I know that, given the way I'm feeling right now, turning on the computer will inevitably lead me to certain websites I should not visit, then maybe I should stay away from the computer (and the smart phones, too!). Hang on to your righteousness and let nothing tear it from your grasp.

Finally, this far into Peter's list of improvements needed we can see that it is not a ladder to climb as we perfect each step, but rather an interconnected group of characteristics, each of which builds off the others. Building my virtue makes self-control easier, but stronger self-control helps me create that excellent character. Both are aided by actively growing in knowledge as deeper understanding of God's perfect word leads to being more virtuous and self-control also becomes easier because temptations will not usually pop-up while one is thinking deeply about God's word. We will see that this continues to be the case as we move through Peter's list. In other words, working on self-improvement aids us as we work on self-improvement. And we're back to quoting Nike: Just do it.

6

In Your Self-Control, Patience

As a kid, I always thought that patience meant not losing your temper. Someone who was patient could deal with constant aggravations and torments without exploding in wrath or losing his cool. That definition is actually much closer to self-control. Patience is another animal altogether. Also translated steadfastness, patience means endurance. It means constancy. It is embodied in the phrase "to keep on keeping on." A patient person does not quit. No matter how hard it becomes, no matter how long it takes, no matter what, the patient person never quits. It is the ethos of the marathon runner: "Therefore, since we are surrounded by so great a cloud of witnesses, let us also lay aside every weight, and sin which clings so closely, and let us run with endurance the race that is set before us" (Heb. 12.1). The word endurance here is the same Greek word that is normally translated patience. We run the race and we keep running it until the race is completed.

Patience is essential to the make-up of a Christian. Throughout the New Testament, in list after list of the traits Christians are to develop, patience is mentioned (e.g., 1 Tim 6.11; 2 Tim 3.10; Titus 2.1–2). God Himself is called the God of patience (Rom 15.5) and we depend upon the patience of Christ (2 Thess 3.5). When we read the letters John wrote for the Lord to the seven churches of Asia, we notice that the phrase "to him that overcomes" is included in each letter and we start to understand that the Christian life is a life of endurance and of overcoming the obstacles that might be in the way. John certainly includes it as an integral part of Christianity: "I John, your brother and partner with you in the tribulation and the kingdom and the patient endurance that are in Jesus" (Rev 1.9). So John, as our partner, partakes with us in three things. These three things must be truly the essence of Christianity. They are tribulation, which falls upon all who believe (2 Tim 3.12), the kingdom which is the church, and patient endurance. When we sign up to be Christians, we must keep on living the Christian life, no matter how hard it gets, or we aren't Christians.

But what is it that we are to endure? The most obvious thing is tribulation, which is just a fancy word for troubles. The troubles Christians must face can be broken down into two categories: persecution and the general afflictions of the world.

As followers of God, we must expect persecution: "Indeed, all who desire to live a godly life in Christ Jesus will be persecuted" (2 Tim 3.12). It is possible that the persecution we face may be for the benefit of other Christians, to edify them by our example (2 Cor 1.6) or it may just be our burden to bear, but as Christians we must bear up under the pressure. Paul praises the Thessalonian church for their patience in persecution: "Therefore we ourselves boast about you in the churches of God for your steadfastness and faith in all your persecutions and in the afflictions that you are enduring" (2 Thess 1.4). In America today we face very little persecution from the government for our faith but that does not mean that we never face any challenges. Our co-workers and neighbors may think we are weird for always attending church or for not participating in all that they do, and may therefore keep us at arm's length. For example, we find out about the office Christmas party the day after. If we dare to maintain that there is such a thing as right and wrong and that some things are unacceptable, that can lead to all sorts of problems. We may be passed over for promotions. We may lose friends. If we were so foolish as to express these standards on social media, we would find ourselves immediately attacked by people we never knew existed. Mean-spirited, judgmental, self-righteous and hypocrite are the nicest things we would be called. If we are not prepared to deal with these things, the fear of them might cause us to stay quiet, to even agree with the wrong to avoid unpleasantness. When we are feeling those temptations, perhaps we should remember Luke 9.26: "For whoever is ashamed of me and of my words, of him will the Son of Man be ashamed when he comes in his glory and the glory of the Father and of the holy angels."

Then there are the normal vicissitudes of the world. Unfortunately, many new converts come into the church with the belief that beginning a new life with Christ means that all our problems will just evaporate. Not only is this not true, but the Bible warns us that we need to be patient in these trials. James holds up Job as an example for us (5.11). I sincerely hope none of us face his problems, yet many things will constantly tug at our faith. Our boss is a jerk, our spouse is moody, our kids get sick and there are more bills to pay than paychecks to cover them. The day-to-day stress can lead us to sin as we look for relief. Then there are bigger problems: a cancer diagnosis or our loved ones pass away or … . In the parable of the sower, Jesus tells of those whose faith fails when they face persecution and tribulations (Matt 13.20–21). It isn't shameful for these things to weigh on us, but the call to patience means we don't let them deter us from our work for Christ.

Patience also calls us to endure as we work for the Lord. Consider 2 Thessalonians 3.13: "As for you, brothers, do not grow weary in doing good." And Galatians 6.9: "And let us not grow weary of doing good, for in due season we will reap, if we do not give up." It might seem odd that this warning exists as we serve our God of love and light, but continually subverting our wills to God and our brethren, sacrificing for others and putting others' needs before our own can start to get old, especially in our society that constantly emphasizes the need for "me time." Our national motto is no longer duty to God, others or principles, but rather "I've got to do what's best for me." With that ethos surrounding us it is easy to "grow weary in doing good." We must watch ourselves and rededicate ourselves to patience in service. God does notice: "to them that by patience in well-doing seek for glory and honor and incorruption, eternal life" (Rom 2.7 ASV).

Besides facing persecution, we might be tempted by other doctrines that please us personally more than God's truth. Whether it be rock-n-roll concerts standing in for worship or the softening of certain prohibitions which would therefore include more of our relatives, it can be awfully tempting to allow changes in the teachings of the Bible. In popular parlance: "Doesn't God want me to be happy?" I'll let God speak:

> "Hold fast the traditions, even as I delivered them to you (1 Cor 11.2 ASV).
>
> "Now I make known unto you brethren, the gospel which I preached unto you, which also you received, wherein also you stand, by which also you are saved, if you hold fast the word which I preached unto you, except ye believed in vain." (1 Cor 15.1-2 ASV)
>
> "So then, brethren, stand fast, and hold the traditions which ye were taught, whether by word, or by epistle of ours." (2 Thess 2.15 ASV)
>
> "Let us hold fast the confession of our hope that it waver not; for he is faithful that promised" (Heb 10.23 ASV)

Is any of that unclear?

Endurance, or patience, is one of the fundamental tenets of the Christian walk. The rewards are great. "To him that overcomes, to him will I give to eat of the tree of life, which is in the Paradise of God" (Rev 2.7 ASV).

7

In Your Patience, Godliness

Quick, if you've ever heard a preacher say that godliness means God-like-ness raise your hands. I'm sure most hands just went up. For a long time, this was the definition that many teachers assigned to this word. Many a sermon has been preached about our need to be imitators of God in order to achieve the state of godliness. The premise of imitating God as best we can in our lives is a good one, after all we are told "Therefore be imitators of God, as beloved children" (Eph 5.1) and "as he who called you is holy, you also be holy in all your conduct" (1 Pet 1.15). So, those old sermons weren't wrong in essence, just in their definition of godliness. If godliness were originally an English word, the definition of God-like-ness might be a valid one. To be friendly is to act like a friend and friendliness is the state of acting like a friend. It is friend-like-ness. The only problem with that analogy to godliness is that the word as originally used was a Greek word, not an English one and we should understand it from the Greek usage rather than by English definitions.

The best way to understand any word is to examine how it is commonly employed in everyday use. This is how dictionaries are written. The Oxford English Dictionary, for example, traces each English word back to the earliest printed usage extant and assigns definitions based on context. This is something that anyone can do with Biblical words. Using free computer programs like e-sword or the Word, or just an old-fashioned bound concordance such as Young's or Strong's anyone can trace the original Greek or Hebrew words through each verse in which it is used and, based on context, come to understand the meanings of these words. Other hints may come from the various English words each original language word is translated into. Before we can discuss how to grow in godliness, we must learn what godliness means. So, we will examine just a few of the many instances of this word in the Bible.

"But know that the LORD has set apart the godly for himself; the LORD hears when I call to him." (Ps 4.3)

I love using the Psalms when trying to understand the meaning of words because the parallelism inherent in Hebrew poetry offers built in definitions, or at least synonyms. (The Greek and Hebrew words translated as "godly" mean the same thing. The Septuagint translators used the same Greek word to translate the Hebrew from the OT that the NT authors use.) In this verse the godly are parallel to those who call upon the LORD. So, the godly are those who pray, who worship, and who rely upon the LORD as well as all the other things that "calling upon the LORD " often encompasses.

"Save, O LORD, for the godly one is gone; for the faithful have vanished from among the children of man." (Ps 12.1)

In this passage, David makes the godly one parallel to the faithful one. So, the godly are those who can be counted upon, especially those who can be relied upon to keep the covenant.

"Preserve my life, for I am godly; save your servant, who trusts in you—you are my God." (Ps 86.2)

Here David parallels his own godliness with serving God. As a servant of God, David trusts in Him. Any servant obeys his master, following his lead. The godly person, then, is a servant of God's who does His will and trusts in Him.

"The godly has perished from the earth, and there is no one upright among mankind." (Mic 7.2)

Poetic parallelism is so much a part of the Hebrew soul that it even works its way into prose writing. In his prophecy, Micah uses "the godly" and the "upright" as synonyms. Therefore, part of godliness is being upright, or righteous, in one's lifestyle.

We could refer to many more passages, in both the Old and New Testaments, but this is enough to give us the basic flavor of the word. From these four passages we see that the godly, or those with the trait of godliness, call unto the LORD. They trust in Him and are faithful to Him. They do His will. Essentially, godliness means living a life towards God. Some have come up with the word godwardness instead of godliness. As forwards means facing the front and moving to the fore, being godward would mean facing towards God in our lives and always moving in His direction. Doesn't that match up with the contextual definition we've uncovered? If my life is about being His servant and doing His will, am I not facing towards God? If I call unto Him with all of my problems and trust in Him, am I not facing towards God? If I am always faithful to Him, am I not facing to God? Godliness is always looking to God to see how He would have us live our lives.

That focus on God and His wishes directs our lives. Those old-time farmers who plowed with mule teams would tell you that if you wanted to plow straight rows, you couldn't just keep your eyes on the south end of the northward moving mule team. You had to focus on the end of the row. They would often put a stake in the ground at the correct point and the whole time they were plowing that row they focused on that stake. That isn't a bad analogy to the Christian life, nor a bad explanation of what godliness really means. If we want to lead a life pleasing to God, a life of righteousness, holiness, love and kindness, then we must keep our focus always on God. We cannot allow the bumpy road of life with all its distractions to move our focus away from God and His desires. Godliness is living our life according to God's will and learning, more and more, to subject our will to His.

Now that we understand godliness how do we grow our godliness? How do we increase our focus on His will rather than ours? Paul wrote quite a bit about this subject to Timothy. In fact, there are more instances of the word godliness in 1 and 2 Timothy than anywhere else in the New Testament: "And exercise yourself unto godliness: for bodily exercise is profitable for a little; but godliness is profitable for all things, having promise of the life which now is, and of that which is to come" (1 Tim 4.7–8 ASV).

Paul equates growth in godliness to exercise. If we want to build our bodies to a higher level of fitness, to have greater stamina or strength, it takes a continued, coordinated effort. We will get sweaty and short of breath. We can't just do it once and expect results, the effort must be regular. We can't swim one day, lift weights the next, then do yoga, then step aerobics, then run. Our bodies will become confused and we will never achieve the stamina or strength we are aiming for. To be better runners we must run regularly. To be stronger we must lift those weights regularly.

Similarly, our efforts to grow in godliness must be continuous and coordinated. Paul instructs Timothy how this exercise should be done. In the lead up to the passage quoted, Paul says to reject false teaching, focusing instead on the good doctrine (vv 1–8). He describes the false doctrine as "seducing"—so it sounds good—but also says that it is spoken by hypocritical men. He calls it "old wives fables" and roundly denounces it as the "doctrine of demons." Learning to recognize and avoid these falsehoods and, instead, be "nourished in the words of the faith, and of the good doctrine" (v 6) is integral to growing our godliness. How can we claim to be focused on God's will if we are seduced by false doctrines? To be focused on God we must know His word, which might just be why Peter mentions knowledge earlier in this list. In 1 Timothy 2.9–10, in discussing the behavior appropriate to women professing godliness, Paul says they should be adorned with good works rather than showy clothes and that their lives be models of sobriety and modesty. It seems apparent to me that if godly women should act like this, then godly men act similarly. How better to exercise my godliness than to be busy with good works? Not to boast, but doing them in modesty because that is the will of God.

Growing in godliness also requires sobriety. Being sober or sober-minded is mentioned 12 times throughout the epistles. This isn't a demand to be joyless automatons, but rather not to be flippant and careless as we walk the pathway of faith. We understand the seriousness of what we are about and we "look carefully how [we] walk" (Eph 5.15). How does this relate to godliness? Because we are focused on doing God's will and are careful to do it.

So, godliness is a focus on and trust in God and what His plan is for us. Growing in that focus is a matter of practice. The more we exercise ourselves in it, by doing good, knowing His word, avoiding false doctrine, and being careful of our walk, the more our godliness will grow.

8

In Your Godliness, Brotherly Kindness

Most discussions of biblical love concentrate on the Greek word *agape*. This word defined in 1 Corinthians 13.4–7 may be the most common word for love in the New Testament, but clearly Peter has something else in mind as he differentiates between love and brotherly kindness. Brotherly kindness in 2 Peter 1.7 is *philadelphia* (which helps explain why the city in Pennsylvania is referred to as "The City of Brotherly Love"). Greek uses four different words for what we think of as love. *Eros* is physical love and passion. *Storge* is the natural, almost chemical love parents have for children. The first time you held your child and were overwhelmed with the need to protect her you were feeling *storge*. This word, rare in the New Testament, is primarily used as a condemnation against those who didn't feel it (e.g. Rom. 1:31 "without natural affection"). Then *agape* is the love of action with very little emotion attached, doing what is best for the one loved. It is the love we can show both close friends and dire enemies. The fourth love is *phileo*, the root of which is used in *philadelphia*. This is family love. It involves some emotion, some affection, but also a strong sense of duty or obligation. After all, brothers fight like cats and dogs sometimes but when one brother sees the other being bullied, we suddenly hear, "Hey! I'm the only one allowed to pick on him!" and the erstwhile adversarial brother is suddenly allied with the tormented one to face the world together. That is *philadelphia*—the idea that blood is thicker than water. It means one drops everything else and runs to help because that is what family does even if I sometimes get so angry at them.

Peter's use of brotherly kindness highlights two points. First, it emphasizes the family bond. We don't just *agape* each other, we *philadelphia*. While we are told clearly that we cannot allow our earthly families to come between us and Christ, that Christ must always come first (Matt 10.37; 19.29), here is our true spiritual family. This is family as it should be. I am aware that I have been very lucky with my family. My father was not only present, which makes him automatically better than about half of fathers, but he actively tried to be the best father he could. Not everyone is so lucky, a prime reason the church as the family of God should be so inviting. Again, family as it should be. A family where we truly love each other. If earthly blood is thicker than water how much thicker still is spiritual blood? This means that all those feelings of duty and obligation we normally feel towards our families should be felt towards our brethren in Christ. If there is need, we drop everything and run to help, because we are family. If others are attacking,

In Your Godliness, Brotherly Kindness | 65

we jump in to defend, because the only one allowed to pick on my spiritual brother is me! Brotherly kindness demands that our spiritual families are now our priority (even over physical family!).

Second, Peter tells us that we can grow in our love for each other, whether *agape* or *philadelphia* and shows us how. He says "give diligence." He later says that if these "are yours and abound" we will not be unfruitful. Diligence means earnest, continuing effort. To abound means to fill to overflowing. We can improve, in fact, one of the most dangerous things a Christian can say is, "that's just how I am". No, that is not *just* how you are! We can grow. The inspired Apostle Peter said so. And no matter how good we are at something there is always room for improvement. In 1 Thessalonians 4.9–10 Paul tells the church that they excel at brotherly love. He holds them up as an example to other churches. After this praise Paul then urges them to continue growing in that area. 'You are the best at this that there is, keep on getting even better'. Romans 12.10, often translated "in honor preferring one another" is translated in the English Standard Version as "outdo one another in showing love." If that latter translation is the most correct, it means that while love does not envy, vaunt itself or seek its own, there is one area in Christianity where there is room for friendly competition: love. I can almost hear the trash talk: "Hey, Bob, I'm going to show you up in love for the brethren"; "Keep dreaming, pal, everyone knows I'm the best at brotherly love in this church!" Silly, perhaps, but imagine a church in which the only competition was who loved best!

No matter how well or how poorly we practice brotherly love at the beginning of our walk with God we can continue to grow in it. As we grow in all these other areas, our love for our brethren will continue to improve as well. We will recognize God's love not only for us but them too. We will recognize our own failures and make allowances for others. Our patience and long-suffering will grow the more we recognize our own struggles, leading to better love of the brethren. The closer we come to Christ, the closer we will feel to His family and the more we will make them a priority. After all, *His* blood is thicker than water.

Social Aspects of Brotherly Love

> "And they devoted themselves to the apostles' teaching and the fellowship, to the breaking of bread and the prayers. And awe came upon every soul, and many wonders and signs were being done through the apostles. And all who believed were together and had all things in common. And they were selling their possessions and belongings and distributing the proceeds to all, as any had need. And day by day, attending the temple together and breaking bread in their homes, they received their food with glad and generous hearts, praising God and having favor with all the people. And the Lord added to their number day by day those who were being saved." (Acts 2.42–47)

We say we want to follow the example of the first century church and model ourselves as nearly as possible after the ancient order of things. This passage describes the first church ever in two ways: devotion to the apostles' teaching and to fellowship. They gathered daily in the temple to learn from the apostles and they took care of each other's needs. Day by day they were in each other's homes, eating together. These people were active in each other's lives. They knew each other and depended on each other. They were a family. These were not people who just nodded at each other with a "Hi, how are you?" once a week.

How well do you know your spiritual family? When I originally preached this as a sermon, I asked some specific questions about certain members to illustrate the point.

1) How do you pronounce _____'s last name? Where is he from?

2) In what field is _____ a certified expert?

3) What is _____'s job? Where does he do it?

4) Did you know that _____ is soon to move? Where is he going?

Obviously, my questions mean nothing to the readers, but you can understand the concept, especially if you try to think of similar questions regarding your own congregation. Do we even know each other? How can we operate as a family if we don't?

There is an elephant in the room that needs to be addressed: the Social Gospel. Many religious organizations recruit new members based on all the social opportunities that the "church" provides. There are sports leagues for the kids, young women's groups, older women's groups, new fathers' groups, regular parties in the fellowship hall, plays, dances, lock-ins and so on and so forth, all paid for by the church—activities for which we have no Biblical authority—and all given as the reason for church attendance. We should not be attending church for the social opportunities, but to worship our God and to serve Him as He directs, yet in divorcing ourselves from the Social Gospel the churches of Christ have nearly gone too far in the other direction, denying any social component in the church. Again I ask, how can we be a family together if we don't know each other?

I submit that we cannot complete our God-given roles if we aren't spending time together. For example, "Therefore, confess your sins to one another and pray for one another, that you may be healed." (Jas 5.16). To do that takes trust and a closeness one doesn't get in a few minutes of chatting in the parking lot each week. To confess your sins is to leave yourself open and vulnerable and will rarely be done with people one doesn't trust. Alcoholics Anonymous achieves this through anonymity. No one knows anyone else there so there can't be any blowback, but in the church we all know each other. So, if I am to confess my failings and weaknesses to a brother, I must know him and trust that he will not gossip or use my confession later as a weapon.

Or consider Romans 12.15: "Rejoice with those who rejoice, weep with those who weep." When something really good happens, you want to share the good news with others, right? You call all your buddies and celebrate together. When was the last time a church member other than immediate physical family was among the first three calls you made? Why not? Because we celebrate with

In Your Godliness, Brotherly Kindness | 69

buddies and I barely know those people I worship with! The same is even more true when mourning. Again, crying makes you vulnerable and is only done among those trusted, not those mere acquaintances at church.

And can I "provoke one another to love and good works" (Heb 10.24) if I don't know in what areas you need exhortation or what type of exhortation works best with you? To know that, we have to know each other.

I could go on, but this seems sufficient to illustrate the point: again and again we cannot perform our God-given duties for our spiritual families if we barely know them. This is not the Social Gospel, but yes, the Gospel does call us to be social. We need to be in each other's homes. We need to meet for lunch. We need to be active in each other's lives.

We will either learn to love each other and our congregations will become spiritual families, or our churches will fail and fall apart. It is that simple.

9

In Your Brotherly Kindness, Love

What does it meant to love my brethren? What does it entail? Do I really have to love them? *All* of them?

The logical place to start any study of love would be 1 Corinthians 13.4–7. In fact, this is an even better place to begin than some might realize, because this passage is *not* talking about romantic love, but love in general. This passage is often read at weddings, and if a man endeavors to love his wife this way and his wife reciprocates the effort, they are guaranteed a long and happy marriage. The context of 1 Corinthians 13, however, is Paul commanding the brethren at Corinth to stop fighting over who has the most prestigious spiritual gifts and learn to work together. Right in the middle of that he gives us this description of love:

> Love is patient and kind; love does not envy or boast; it is not arrogant or rude. It does not insist on its own way; it is not irritable or resentful; it does not rejoice at wrongdoing, but rejoices with the truth. Love bears all things, believes all things, hopes all things, endures all things.

The first thing you should notice is that love, as defined by the Bible, is not an emotion. Love is not warm, mushy feelings nor is it wild, passionate desires. Love, as taught by the inspired Apostle, is action. Love is what I do, or refrain from doing, for the one I love. If I say I love someone but I am not patient and kind but rather arrogant and rude toward them, then I don't really love them. Not the way the Bible describes love. According to Paul, I can have warm, mushy feelings towards someone and not love them while disliking someone else and still loving them. This is how we can follow Jesus' command to love our enemies (Matt 5.44). I don't have to like them—if they are my enemies and continue to "spitefully use" me, I probably don't like them—but I can love them by treating them as described above.

A second thing to notice about this list is how often patience of one kind or another comes up. "Love is patient" or long-suffering as older translations say. It is not irritable but does bear all things and endure all things. That's four out of fifteen descriptions. How much of loving someone is just putting up with them? Honestly, you people married 30 years or more, how much of the reason you are still together is you've learned just to put up with each other? Certainly, you are fond of each other and do nice things for each other and rely on each other, but if you hadn't learned to overlook a few things over the years, you might not be together now would you? If that is true of a marriage, wouldn't it also be true of my relationship with my brother in Christ? Be patient.

Finally, "believes all things, hopes all things" means that I don't automatically assume that everything my brother says or does is mean-spirited and meant to hurt me. Instead, I believe the opposite: that my brother would never intentionally hurt me or undermine me. "He must have misspoken." "I must have misunderstood his meaning." We will give every possible benefit of the doubt. If more Christians believed and hoped all things about their brethren, there would be a lot less fighting in the church.

Love of and for the brethren is a concept much discussed in the New Testament. Learning to live the concepts in 1 Corinthians 13.4–7 is a good way to begin.

Why should I love my brethren?

Let's be honest, some of you aren't very lovable. I'm even less so. As we have learned, the Bible defines love as action. Things we do for those we love, or things we refrain from. If we must work so hard to love one another, there had better be a good reason. Otherwise, we might just sit this one out.

So, why should we? Here's one reason: love is fundamental to Christianity. John 13.34–35 tells us that love of the brethren is a command from Christ. More than that, our love for each other is the identifier of His disciples. If Christ's followers are known by their love for each other, and we don't love our brethren, are we really a followers of Christ? Also, the Apostle John tells us that love for the brethren was one of the foundational commands of early Christianity. It was the "message … heard from the beginning" (1 John 3.11) and "the commandment …

heard from the beginning" (2 John 5–6). Paul tells us in that love of the brethren has always been a basic tenet of God's people (Gal 5.14). After all, the entire Law of Moses could be summed up by "love thy neighbor."

A second reason to love your brothers is that you cannot have a relationship with God without loving them. After all, "Anyone who does not love does not know God" (1 John 4.8). And "If anyone says, 'I love God,' and hates his brother, he is a liar; for he who does not love his brother whom he has seen cannot love God whom he has not seen" (1 John 4.20). The only way to have a successful relationship with God is to love your brethren. In fact, love of the brethren almost defines our relationship with God. "if we love one another, God abides in us and his love is perfected in us" (1 John 4.12).

To walk with Christ is to love the brethren. "This is my commandment, that you love one another as I have loved you…. You are my friends if you do what I command you" (John 15.12,14). In other words, you can't be a friend of Jesus' if you don't love the brethren. Also, the only way to know we are of the truth is to love one another (1 John 3.18–19).

So, love of the brethren is a central concept of Christianity, necessary to having relationships with both the Father and the Son, and the only true way to know if I am of the truth. There is one other reason to love my brethren: to be ready for the judgment. Consdier 1 Peter 4.7–8: "The end of all things is at hand; therefore be self-controlled and sober-minded for the sake of your prayers. Above all, keep loving one another earnestly."

The end is near and Peter tells us that the most important thing I can do to get ready for judgment is to love my brethren. The most important thing I can do to get ready for judgment is to love my brethren. Ok, ok, maybe I'll try to love you unlovable rascals.

Love Expressed as Hospitality

> The end of all things is at hand; therefore be self-controlled and sober-minded for the sake of your prayers. Above all, keep loving one another earnestly, since love covers a multitude of sins. Show hospitality to one another without grumbling. As each has received a gift, use it to serve one another, as good stewards of God's varied grace. (1 Pet 4.7–10)

The last section ended with this passage, but let's take a closer look. The first thing to note about this passage is the urgency behind it. "The end of all things is at hand." Peter clearly didn't mean "soon to happen" because it has been 2,000 years and the end hasn't happened yet, but for millennia people were looking forward to the coming of the Messiah. Now that He has come there is nothing else happening between us and the end, which will come "like a thief in the night". Given that we must be ready. Peter tells us three things to do: be self-controlled, sober minded, and love one another earnestly. Peter emphasizes that of these, love is the most important. "Above all" love one another. Love is then broken down into two endeavors: covering a multitude of sins and showing hospitality to one another. First, let's focus on hospitality.

In the 20th and now the 21st centuries we have come to think of hospitality as having people over for dinner or socializing with each other in a variety of ways. That really has nothing to do with the concept of hospitality at the time Peter wrote his epistle. This is not to say that getting to know one another socially is not important. In the chapter on brotherly kindness, we have already discussed the importance of knowing one another socially. Socializing is important, but it is not what Peter meant by hospitality.

The International Standard Bible Encyclopedia (ISBE) says that hospitality was a duty in the ancient days when travelers had nowhere to stay. Hosts often took in strangers and cared for them. It was considered an honor to be allowed to provide in this way. According to the ISBE there were four main components to Eastern hospitality:

1) The traveler is made the literal master of the house during his stay.

2) The host performs the most servile offices for the traveler and won't even sit in the presence of the traveler.

3) The guest is given use of all the host owns, including even the host's wife and daughters. (The last is not Biblical nor condoned in any way by Biblical teaching, but it does show the devotion the ancients had to hospitality.)

4) The host is duty bound to protect the guest from all dangers that may arise during his stay.

We have Biblical examples of all these precepts, which is not surprising since hospitality was held in such high regard that Job defined his righteousness in part by his devotion to hospitality (Job 31.32).

In Genesis 18.1–8 we have the story of Abraham showing hospitality to three strangers. He runs to meet them, begs for the right to serve them and, despite promising only a drink of water and a bit of bread, provides cakes made with the finest flour and a young calf cooked—think veal—as well as milk and butter. While they are eating, Abraham stands by ready to serve. He doesn't join them in eating in his own camp. He stands by like a servant.

In Judges 19 a Levite is traveling and when he gets to a Benjaminite town, no one will take him in. When someone finally speaks to him, he offers, out of desperation, to pay his own way for the right to not sleep in the streets, which offer normally would have been a deadly insult. The older man speaking to him says, ""Peace be to you; I will care for all your wants. Only, do not spend the night in the square" (vv 15–21). While the town failed in its duties, the old man accomplished hospitality by providing for all the needs of the traveler.

Then a truly shameful thing happens (vv 22–23). The men of the city try to attack the traveling Levite. True to his duties as host, the old man steps out and faces the crowd, protecting his guest: "do not act so wickedly; since this man has come into my house." If this sounds familiar it is because it is an almost exact replay of what happened in Sodom when Lot tried to protect the men who were staying with him.

It is this level of hospitality which Peter commands in 1 Peter 4.9. Instead of being good to strangers, though, he says to show hospitality "to one another." The ASV says "among yourselves." So, we should adapt these principles to our relationships with our brethren.

1) The guest becomes master of the house. Galatians 5.13 tells us that we should "through love be servants one to another". I should be acting as if my brothers are the bosses and I provide their needs. I stand by to wait upon them. Philippians 2.4 reminds us not to look out for ourselves but to look out for the needs of our brothers. My first thought is not "what is best for me", but rather "what is best for my brethren?" If everyone does this, all will be taken care of, and we will be showing hospitality.

2) The host performs the most servile offices for the guest. Washing guests' feet was among the most demeaning services rendered and the task was usually given the servant with the least status. That shows why the Apostles were so shocked when Jesus began washing their feet in John 13. He then explains, "If I then, your Lord and Teacher, have washed your feet, you also ought to wash one another's feet" (v 14). In other words, there is nothing my brother might need from me that I am too important to do. Repeat: *there is nothing my brother might need from me that I am too important to do.* This is love.

3) The guest is given access to all the host owns. 1 John 3.16 says we ought to be willing to die for our brethren. Romans 8.32 says that God, having already sacrificed His Son for us is willing to give us anything else we might need. If you put those concepts together, then if I am willing to die for my brothers is there anything short of dying that I'd withhold from them? In a way, even to the point of sharing your spouse. Ask any Elder's wife or preacher's wife if she doesn't share her husband with the church. And some husbands, whose wives are the older women who teach the younger (Titus 2) or who are best at weeping with those who weep also share their spouses with the church. Why do these brothers and sisters put up with the disruptions to their home life? Because they are showing hospitality through love.

4) The host is duty bound to protect the guest from all dangers. If I am to protect my brethren from dangers and I know there is a lion stalking the earth trying to eat them (1 Pet 5.8) what should I be protecting them from? Isn't it my responsibility as a hospitable brother to do what I can to protect my brethren from the temptations of Satan? Certainly, I should not be putting stumbling blocks in front of them (Matt 18.7). So, if I usually have a glass of wine with a meal, but I know my brother is a recovering alcoholic, I shouldn't pour him a glass of wine when he comes over for dinner. I probably shouldn't even drink my glass in front of him. And while it is every man's responsibility to control his own thoughts and eyes, surely if my sister loves me, she won't dress in such a way as to excite illicit thoughts. Why do you think the most common adjective used to describe clothes these days is "sexy"? Because those clothes are designed to provoke certain responses. I submit that no Christian woman *or man* should be wearing clothes that are *designed* to be sexy. Attractive? yes. Nice looking? yes. Sexy? no. Not if I love my sisters and my sisters love me. Or if there is anything else I might do to put a temptation in front of a brother, I need to be willing to give those things up (1 Cor 8.13).

Loving through hospitality is serving my brethren, giving my all for my brethren, and protecting my brethren. Is this really that important? In the judgment scene in Matthew 25 those saved are those who hospitably served their brethren and those sent into outer darkness are those who didn't serve. It is interesting that holiness, righteousness nor godliness are mentioned in this scene at all but rather service. Yes, it's important.

Love Covers Sins

> The end of all things is at hand; therefore be self-controlled and sober-minded for the sake of your prayers. Above all, keep loving one another earnestly, since love covers a multitude of sins. Show hospitality to one another without grumbling. As each has received a gift, use it to serve one another, as good stewards of God's varied grace. (1 Pet 4.7–10)

Again, note the urgency: "the end is at hand." But what does it mean that love covers a multitude of sins?

First, it is not referring to covering up sins against God. Everything in the Bible teaches against that. Paul declares that the unrepentant sinner is to be expelled from the church (1 Cor 5.1–8). Clearly that means confronting sin, not covering it up. Jesus' letter to the church in Thyatira in Revelation 2.20 mentions that the only thing He had against that church was that they tolerated a false teacher. Obviously, He had expected them to confront that sinner. Instead of covering sins up, we are encouraged to bring the sinner to repentance. Galatians

6.1 tells us to go to the sinner, 2 Thessalonians 3.15 tells us to admonish the sinner, and James 5.19–20 speaks of converting the sinner. None of this "covers" the sins.

So, what does it mean? Look at the proverb Peter quotes: "Hatred stirs up strifes but love covers all transgressions" (Prov 10.12 ASV). While hatred looks for ways to cause problems, love seeks to build the relationship; to build trust. Love overlooks, or covers, all the transgressions of the loved one against the lover. In other words, the sins covered by love are the offenses or transgressions my brethren perpetrate against me. If someone is rude to me it may not be sin in the evil-against-God sense, but I have still been offended. To transgress is to cross a line, which is instructive. If I love people, then when they cross a line with me, I overlook it.

Of course, sometimes the transgression is serious and needs to be addressed. Jesus gives us the method to do this in Matthew 18.15–17: "If your brother sins against you, go and tell him his fault, between you and him alone. If he listens to you, you have gained your brother. But if he does not listen, take one or two others along with you, that every charge may be established by the evidence of two or three witnesses. If he refuses to listen to them, tell it to the church. And if he refuses to listen even to the church, let him be to you as a Gentile and a tax collector." These are the rights of the offended brother with the goal always being to regain your brother. However, notice the seriousness of the consequences. If your brother is too stubborn to apologize and make things right, he can wind up cut off from the church.

That means there can be eternal consequences for an offense which may not have been evil to begin with. As the offended party, were you hurt so badly to chance that outcome, or will you allow your love for your brother to cover the transgressions? Paul teaches us that in order to keep the peace within the church we ought to be willing to be wronged, to let love cover those wrongs: "No, already it is altogether a defect in you, that you have lawsuits one with another. Why not rather take wrong? Why not rather be defrauded?" (1 Cor 6.7 ASV).

Love covering a multitude of sins means forgiveness. We aren't keeping track of the transgressions to make use of later. Love "takes no account of evil" (1 Cor 13.5 ASV). That phrase is actually the same phrase used by first century Greeks to mean bookkeeping in business. We don't "keep book" of others' sins against us. We forgive. Forgiveness must be genuine. If I forgive, but then refuse to speak to the offender I haven't really forgiven. If I forgive, but speak ill of or make sure to sit on the opposite side of the building or refuse all requests from that brother, that isn't forgiveness. In those cases I'm not covering sins but quietly hoarding injustices to myself. If we can, we should always choose to overlook insults, but if the offense is egregious then we *must* use the steps Jesus gives in Matthew 18. These are the only two options given Christians by God. Quietly stewing is not an option.

"Love suffers long". Most offenses we deal with from our brethren are minor in reality but annoying personally. If I love that brother, I put up with it. Maybe I address it, maybe not, but either way I love my brother. And remember, love "believes all things and hopes all things." I will not assume my brother is out to get me, but rather is just innocently annoying.

Finally, allow me to let you in on a secret: we are all annoying. None of us are perfect in everything. *you* annoy someone greatly. God loves us despite our annoying tendencies and teaches us to love in the same way. One day the annoyances will be gone forever while "love never ends" (1 Cor 13.8).

10

The Works of the Flesh vs. the Fruit of the Spirit

Peter isn't the only New Testament writer to discuss Christian growth. In his discussion of the fruit of the spirit, Paul outlines several traits that we should be harvesting if we are living by the spirit. Obviously, growth in these areas is expected. Before he jumps into that topic of growth, however, Paul examines a more fundamental aspect of human nature that impacts our discussion of growth. He asks the question, "Are we of the flesh or of the spirit?"

> But I say, walk by the Spirit, and you will not gratify the desires of the flesh. For the desires of the flesh are against the Spirit, and the desires of the Spirit are against the flesh, for these are opposed to each other, to keep you from doing the things you want to do. But if you are led by the Spirit, you are not under the law. (Gal 5.16–18)

First in the original, the "s" is Spirit wasn't capitalized. Or, more accurately, all the letters were capitalized as lowercase letters were not invented yet. In either case, the passage contains no indication that Paul refers here to the Holy Spirit. Instead, he discusses man's dual nature and encourages us to follow after spiritual things rather than fleshly things.

The duality of man cannot be denied. This fact is discussed throughout the Bible and can be traced all the way back to Creation. It was from the dust of the ground that man was formed (Gen 2.7), but in verse 19 we learn that the animals were also formed from the ground. In other words, the body of man was created from the same material as the animals and we have the same fleshly desires and passions that the animals do: hunger, thirst, procreation, territoriality, pain and anger, among others. What makes man different from the animals is also found in Genesis 2.7: "then the Lord God … breathed into his nostrils the breath of life, and the man became a living creature." We were created in the same manner as the animals, but we have an element of the divine as God breathed life into us. Part of us is eternal and that part is aware that there are deeper issues than merely fulfilling each passing bodily desire: "He has put eternity into man's heart" (Ecc 3.11).

The desires of the flesh are not inherently evil. God created them. He declared that all He had created was "very good" (Gen 1.31). Each of those desires may be fulfilled in God-approved ways. We can enjoy the good meals that God blesses us with without becoming gluttons. We can protect our families and property without becoming hate-filled souls set on revenge and murder. We are encouraged to enjoy the God-given wonders of sex within the God-given institution of marriage. (And if you don't think "encouraged" is the right word, read the Song of Solomon. It isn't an allegory, it's a passionate poem of romance.) These desires don't become sin until we pervert them and act upon them in ways outside of God's design.

Truly the problem isn't the desires of the flesh themselves, but our mindset toward them. In Romans 8.5 Paul says, "For those who live according to the flesh set their minds on the things of the flesh, but those who live according to the spirit set their minds on the things of the spirit." The question really becomes, "What am I led by?" Is my life focused on my spiritual nature, looking to things of eternity, or am I led by the fleshly desires of my body and the temporary fulfillments of the flesh? As you continue reading in Romans 8, you can see that the whole mindset of those led by the flesh is askew: "For to set the mind on the flesh is death, but to set the mind on the Spirit is life and peace. For the mind that is set on the flesh is hostile to God, for it does not submit to God's law; indeed, it cannot. Those who are in the flesh cannot please God" (vv 6–8). Hostile to God, cannot submit to His law, cannot please God; truly we understand why Paul begins by saying that to be led by the flesh is death. This mindset focuses on earthly things, the needs of the flesh, rather than on heavenly things (Phil 3.19). Those with this mindset focus on personal security, filling up those 401Ks and Roth IRAs. They are immersed in their children's earthly success. They focus on things of this world, forgetting that there is a world to come and in doing so, they fall prey to the sinful works of the flesh:

"Now the works of the flesh are evident: sexual immorality, impurity, sensuality, idolatry, sorcery, enmity, strife, jealousy, fits of anger, rivalries, dissensions, divisions, envy, drunkenness, orgies, and things like these. I warn you, as I warned you before, that those who do such things will not inherit the kingdom of God." (Gal 5.19–21)

Those led by the spirit look beyond fleshly things and desires. They control those desires and keep the fulfillment of them in the proper spheres. People led by the spirit focus on the eternal realm: "If then you have been raised with Christ, seek the things that are above, where Christ is, seated at the right hand of God. Set your minds on things that are above, not on things that are on earth" (Col 3.1–2). Because they have this focus, people led by the spirit will do things inexplicable to the worldly. Abraham was willing to sacrifice his son (Gen 22) and Stephen preached the truth knowing it would likely lead to his death (Acts 7). The one whose focus is on things above will give up all to follow the spiritual way and please God.

This leads us to the fruit of the spirit as listed by Paul. And notice that it is fruit, not fruits. This also differentiates it from the fleshly things. There are the works (plural) of the flesh, but the fruit (singular) of the spirit. Each of us have different temptations. There are many works of the flesh. All who follow after the spiritual things, however, can reap the fruit of the spirit. The various qualities listed by Paul are all aspects of the fruit of the spirit and all those with a spiritual mindset have access to the totality of the fruit. We may each be tempted only by some of the works of the flesh. All of us, though, can reap the full harvest of the fruit of the spirit: love *and* joy *and* peace *and* patience *and* kindness *and* goodness *and* faithfulness *and* meekness *and* self-control.

Since God expects us to harvest fruit in each of these areas, we must be nurturing our souls to grow in them. As I'm sure you have noticed, quite a few of these aspects of the fruit of the spirit were also mentioned by Peter. We will skip those and focus on the newer areas not already discussed.

> But the fruit of the Spirit is love, joy, peace, patience, kindness, goodness, faithfulness, gentleness, self-control; against such things there is no law. (Gal 5.22–23)

11

Joy

Strong's defines joy as "cheerfulness and calm delight." While not incorrect, let's emphasize the gulf between joy and happiness. Happiness is a temporary emotion based on circumstance. Joy can be your mindset for life. Joy can be experienced during affliction (1 Thess 1.6), but never happiness.

As to happiness: have you ever heard someone say, as they justify why they are acting in contravention to God's word, "Well, God would want me to be happy, right? and this makes me happy"? To those who think that way, read about the lives of Job, Jeremiah and Ezekiel. Examine the service of John the Baptizer and of Paul and tell me again how much God worried about their happiness. The Lord says we must deny ourselves (Mark 8.34). We must subject ourselves to the will of the brethren (Eph 5.21) and put others first (Phil 2.4). I submit that God doesn't really care how happy you are here on this Earth. He is far too busy ensuring that we experience joy for all eternity. And which would you rather possess: a temporary emotion or an eternal state of being?

Adam Clarke defines joy as "The exultation that arises from a sense of God's mercy communicated to the soul in the pardon of its iniquities, and the prospect of that eternal glory of which it has the foretaste in the pardon of sin." From this definition, we see how one might continue to joy even in times of persecution and affliction. Even in the midst of agony or angst, we remember God's mercy and our resulting prospect of eternal glory and we rejoice. Since nothing can separate us from the love of God (Rom 8.35–38), no temporary circumstance can take away our joy.

Albert Barnes doesn't so much define joy as he lists the things that can bring us joy: "in love of God; in the evidence of pardon; in communion with the Redeemer, and in His service; in the duties of religion, in trial, and in the hope of heaven." Mr. Barnes' list closely parallels many Biblical passages about joy. We find joy in God's protection (Ps 5.11) and in His presence (Ps. 16.11) and strength (Ps 21.1). We feel joy in the opportunity to worship and commune with God (Ps 42.4) and in the opportunity to do righteousness (Prov 21.15). And so on and so forth. With a God of holiness, justice, kindness and longsuffering, a God of love, we find ample reasons for joy.

Understanding that the ultimate basis for our joy is our salvation from Hell and the promise of glory to come might affect our reading of 1 John 5.13: "I write these things to you who believe in the name of the Son of God, that you may know that you have eternal life." Knowing that we have eternal life is the source of joy. John says he is writing to those with faith to confirm that knowledge. One thing we can surmise from this passage is that growing faith combined with growing knowledge leads to growing joy. Here is another example of how all of these areas for Christian personal growth are interconnected as we see two of the first three items studied deeply entwined with the ninth area. Faith requires some knowledge upon which to base the faith, but long-term growth in faith also requires an understanding of our joy, or we will just cease our efforts. Joy requires both faith and knowledge for continued growth. Joy, of course, buttresses our next topic, peace.

12

Peace

Strong's defines peace as quietness and rest. We most often consider peace the absence of war, the cessation of open hostilities. This is not Biblical peace. The Lord Himself refutes this: "Do not think that I have come to bring peace to the earth. I have not come to bring peace, but a sword. For I have come to set a man against his father, and a daughter against her mother, and a daughter-in-law against her mother-in-law. And a person's enemies will be those of his own household" (Matt 10.34–36). Far from peace, Jesus warns that following Him will lead to strife, even among our own families. So, what is the peace in the fruit of the Spirit?

Adam Clarke defines this peace as "the calm, quiet and order which takes place in the justified soul instead of the doubts, fears, alarms and dreadful forebodings ... Peace is the first sensible [meaning detectable to the senses] fruit of the pardon of sin." The blessing of this is sorely needed in our modern society. Did you know that the number one class of prescribed medicines in the U.S. is antidepressants? That it has been that way for decades? And how many millions more self-medicate with alcohol or various illegal drugs, from marijuana to heroin? Even nonbelievers recognize a lack in their lives. Even if we don't call it sin, everyone recognizes that we have all done bad things that have hurt others, and that we can do nothing to fix it. We may apologize, and they may accept our apology, but at some level we all know that "I'm sorry" just isn't good enough. That weighs on our minds. Then arises the mid-life crisis when we come to emotionally understand what we've always intellectually known: we won't live forever. The time comes when we won't be here anymore. If we are honest, by the time we have that revelation we have lived longer already than we have time left. Eternity's night is facing and, in reality, none of us will be remembered beyond one generation. Facing that end leads many to sleepless nights and jittery days. Mr. Clarke's definition again: "the calm, quiet and order which takes place in the justified soul instead of the doubts, fears, alarms and dreadful forebodings ... Peace is the first sensible fruit of the pardon of sin."

Perhaps the best—and maybe the most predictable—passage concerning peace is Philippians 4.6–7 "do not be anxious about anything, but in everything by prayer and supplication with thanksgiving let your requests be made known to God. And the peace of God, which surpasses all understanding, will guard your hearts and your minds in Christ Jesus." Paul says this peace surpasses all understanding. In other words, the world sees our peace and can't understand how we have achieved it. Our peace amazes them. We are reminded of 1 Peter 3.15: "always being prepared to make a defense to anyone who asks you for a reason for the hope that is in you." People see the hope in us by the way we live our lives and ask us about it, not understanding. In the same way our peace surpasses their understanding unless we teach them of our Gospel hope.

Even with our knowledge of God's plan of salvation, fear of our sins and failures can overwhelm our peace. How do we grow that peace? How can we harvest this bit of the fruit of the spirit? The answer lies in the first of the two verses quoted above. "Do not be anxious about anything, but in everything by prayer and supplication with thanksgiving let your requests be made known to God" (Phil 4.6). We don't hold on to all the little niggling, nagging worries. We turn them over to God. Instead of being anxious, we pray and bring our supplication to Him. This isn't a grudging concession from the All-Mighty God. Instead, He wants us to bring our problems to Him. "Humble yourselves, therefore, under the mighty hand of God so that at the proper time he may exalt you, casting all your anxieties on him, because he cares for you" (1 Pet 5.6–7). He cares for us. He wants to help. We trust in Him. In our faith we find peace.

We do this "with thanksgiving". As we bring our worries and anxieties to God, we remember to thank Him for all He has done. It is easier to let go of the current worries when I am reminded of all the good that God has already done for me as I offer thanks. Giving thanks for forgiveness, adoption, redemption, grace, etc. causes the temporal problems we are plagued with to dissolve away into the eternal calm of God's peace.

13

Kindness and Goodness

Kindness and goodness are closely related concepts and somewhat self-explanatory so we will treat both together in one chapter.

Kindness, also translated throughout the New Testament as goodness and gentleness, is a divine trait. The kindness of God leads us to repentance (Rom 2.4). God showcases the greatness of His grace by His kindness (Eph 2.7). God's kindness is reserved for those, of any race, who live by their faith (Rom 11.20, 22) and His kindness heals our sin-sick souls. When we understand the fruit of the spirit to mean the harvest gathered from a life focused upon the spiritual path, rather than the desires of the flesh, then we see that this produce of the spirit puts us into contact with the kindness of God.

However, the fruit of the spirit is usually understood to be traits which we ourselves can grow. Kindness is a trait we can learn, truly a blessing because, while some are born with an almost inherent sense of kindness, many of us really have to work at being kind. We can learn it, however, and we will see in the upcoming passages that

Kindness and Goodness | 95

kindness, like all the traits we have discussed so far, is not based on emotionalism or our inner opinions of others. Kindness is what we do, how we treat others.

> All have turned aside; together they have become worthless; no one does good, not even one. (Rom 3.12)

Here Paul quotes Psalms 14. In this poetic passage, "All have turned aside; together they have become worthless" is parallel to "no one does good". "Does good" is our word for kindness. So, becoming worthless to God, or unprofitable as the ASV translates it, occurs when we act unkindly. This really emphasizes the importance of growing in kindness. The last thing we want is the Creator viewing us as worthless.

> "For my yoke is easy, and my burden is light." (Matt 11.30)

"Wait a second," I can already hear some of you saying, "kindness is not even mentioned in this passage!" Reading it in English you are correct. Kindness is not mentioned. But the word translated "easy" is the same Greek word that everywhere else is translated kindness, goodness or gentleness. It could read 'my yoke is kind, my burden is light'. So, what makes the burden of Christ easy or kind? It is light. It does not overburden us. So, what is one way I can learn to be more kind? I don't overburden my friends. Paul famously teaches that love "bears all things" (1 Cor 13.7), but kindness keeps me from making my friends carry too much. I don't expect others to handle all the hard stuff while I skip through life like a child. Surely we can all come to understand that there is a difference between "get[ting] by with a little help from my friends" and being overly needy.

> "Be kind to one another, tenderhearted, forgiving one another, as God in Christ forgave you." (Eph 4.32)

As Paul expounds upon what it means to be kind to one another, he mentions two things: being tenderhearted and forgiving one another. If I am kind, then when my brother wrongs me, I don't blow up in wrath. I don't give him a piece of my mind or read him the riot act. In my tenderheartedness I am inclined to overlook such things. In my kindness, I am looking for the opportunity to forgive him.

> "But love your enemies, and do good, and lend, expecting nothing in return, and your reward will be great, and you will be sons of the Most High, for he is kind to the ungrateful and the evil." (Luke 6.35)

Doing good is equated with being kind like God is kind. These good works as laid out by Jesus include loving enemies and lending with no expectation of getting back that which was lent. In other words, we are to be kind to even the unthankful and evil. So, my being kind is not a matter of who the recipient is, but of who I am. I am to do good, be kind, because I am a kind, good person. Period. In fact, we become closer to God's ideal when we are kind to those who least deserve it.

Paul then adds the word goodness to the description of the fruit of the spirit. Since the word for kindness is also often translated goodness, clearly those concepts are related. This is a different word, however. Paul didn't stutter. There must be some distinction, however small.

Adam Clarke defines this word as "the desire to not only abstain from sin, but actively to do good." We aren't just avoiding the thou shalt nots, we are actively obeying the thou shalts also. A couple of passages might help us in understanding some of the nuances of this concept.

> "And I myself also am persuaded of you, my brethren, that you yourselves are full of goodness, filled with all knowledge, able also to admonish one another." (Rom 15.14 ASV)

> "...for the fruit of the light is in all goodness and righteousness and truth." (Eph 5.9 ASV)

See how in these passages goodness accompanies knowledge, righteousness and truth. Righteousness is a legal term meaning, essentially, to follow the rules. So, goodness is linked with obtaining a knowledge of the truth and living by that knowledge. This is goodness according to a divine standard, not goodness according to what feels right or what society tells us is right. The Biblical trait of goodness means learning what God declares to be good and then living by that standard.

And again we see the interlocking nature of all these traits.

14

Faithfulness

"Faithfulness" in Galatians 5.22 is the same word translated "faith" throughout most of the New Testament, *pistis*. However, we have already discussed faith extensively and so, even though it isn't the actual word used here, we will take this opportunity to discuss faithfulness. *Pistos* is often translated "trustworthy" and we can gain a great understanding of this concept by tracing its usage.

The Hebrew words *emun* and *emunah*, most often translated "faithful" or "trustworthy," literally mean to be steady. In Exodus 17, when Moses desperately needed to keep his staff above his head so that the Israelites would win their battle with the Amalekites, Aaron and Hur stood on either side of him to brace his arms and "his hands were steady" (v 12). That's our word, steady or faithful. Isaiah uses this word to speak of a building's foundation (33.6), something else that is steady, and can counted upon. That literal meaning of steadiness came to be used of jobs of responsibility (1 Chron 9.22) which clearly needed steady, trustworthy men filling them, and of the faithful completion of an office of trust (2 Chron 31.12). This person completed his job honestly, with no embezzlement or careless loss.

It is easy to see how this word came to be used of people who could be counted upon. In Proverbs 14.5 we see the faithful witness, who could be counted on to speak the truth and in Proverbs 13.17 the faithful envoy who could be counted on to complete tasks of immense importance correctly. Psalm 119.75 mentions that God was being faithful when He afflicted the psalmist, according to His righteous judgments. Not that God wanted to afflict this man, but He was faithful even in an unpleasant task: His duty according to His promise in the Sinatic Covenant. This reminds me of 1 Peter 3.9–10: God delays His judgment hoping that everyone will repent, but He will indeed come. He is faithful even in the things He'd rather not do, and we are also called to this level of faithfulness. In the New Testament, Jesus several times uses the image of a faithful servant saying that this person can be counted on to fulfill his duties (Luke 12.42) and is trustworthy with valuable things (Matt 25.21). So, if we are faithful, in any endeavor, people know that they can count on us to do the job, to fulfill the responsibilities, and to be honest in our dealings. Christianity leads us to be faithful to the covenant we have with God, the "perfect law of liberty" (Jas 1.25).

We can grow in this trait of faithfulness or trustworthiness. The psalmist says, "I have chosen the way of faithfulness" (119.30) and thus faithfulness is a choice. Psalm 89.2 says that God will establish His faithfulness. A quality of faithfulness is that it can be established. So, we can choose to be faithful and establish, or fix, that trait in our lives. Someone said that a journey of one thousand miles begins with a single step, and our journey to faithfulness begins with the decision to fix it solidly in our lives.

In Psalm 37.3, David says that we should feed upon the Lord's faithfulness. What happens when we feed on something? We take it into ourselves; it becomes a part of who we are. If we eat nothing but sugar, we become hyper and jittery and, eventually, diabetic. Ingesting too much fat clogs our arteries and makes us fat. To build muscle we must consume protein (usually animal muscle) and exercise. We become what we consume. If we are spiritually feeding on God's faithfulness—thinking about it and how it applies in so many areas; trying to learn how to live similarly ourselves, in short, meditating on Him—then we also will become faithful. Feeding upon the faithfulness of the Lord is a lifelong process, but similar processes will help us in each of the areas we are discussing. "Therefore, be imitators of God" (Eph 5.1).

Psalm 89:33 shows us that it is possible, if we so choose, to be false to our faithfulness. In other words, we can stop being faithful. The temptation to sin, to take that which has been entrusted to us or to be slothful and not complete our tasks, can always rear its ugly head. We must constantly be on guard, feeding on His faithfulness because only he "that keeps faith may enter in" to the gates of the Lord (Isa. 26.2).

15

Meekness

In an effort to avoid the pat definition I've heard all my life (strength under control), I examined every instance of meek or meekness in the Old and New Testaments, trying to define the word based on contextual use.

First, and I'm sure we all know this, meekness does not equal weakness. Moses, "the meekest man on the earth" (Num 12.3), ground up the golden calf, put it in the drinking water and made the Israelites drink it. He then drew a line in the sand and called for volunteers to help him slaughter those who had sinned against God. Three thousand men were executed. Meekness is not weakness. We find further proof in Psalms 45:4 "In your majesty ride out victoriously for the cause of truth and meekness and righteousness; let your right hand teach you awesome deeds!" A psalm about a human king who can ride in majesty and prosperity because of his meekness. We don't normally think of meekness and majesty going together, but there it is.

Meekness doesn't mean gentleness either. Three different Hebrew words are translated meek or meekness. The primary word (*anav*) is also translated humble, lowly, and poor, but not once gentleness. Only one of the other words is ever translated gentleness and that only once. If you think about it, the idea of gentleness doesn't really jive with Moses' actions or those of a majestic king. Let's look at some passages and see what we can figure out.

> "The meek shall eat and be satisfied; They shall praise Jehovah that seek after him: Let your heart live for ever." (Ps 22.26 ASV)

Again, the great thing about doing word studies in the Psalms is that the parallelism inherent in Hebrew poetry essentially defines the words for us. Here the meek are parallel with those that seek after Jehovah.

> "For evil-doers shall be cut off; But those that wait for Jehovah, they shall inherit the land. For yet a little while, and the wicked shall not be: Yea, thou shalt diligently consider his place, and he shall not be. But the meek shall inherit the land, And shall delight themselves in the abundance of peace." (Ps 37.9–11 ASV)

Here, those who wait for Jehovah are parallel with the meek.

> "The meek also shall increase their joy in Jehovah, and the poor among men shall rejoice in the Holy One of Israel." (Isa 29.19 ASV)

> "Seek Jehovah, all you meek of the earth, that have kept his ordinances; seek righteousness, seek meekness: it may be you will be hid in the day of Jehovah's anger" (Zeph 2.3 ASV)

> "For Jehovah takes pleasure in his people: He will beautify the meek with salvation. Let the saints exult in glory: Let them sing for joy upon their beds." (Ps 149.4–5 ASV)

So, the meek joy in Jehovah, keep His ordinances, and are called His people and saints.

> "And Miriam and Aaron spoke against Moses because of the Cushite woman whom he had married; for he had married a Cushite woman. And they said, Has Jehovah indeed spoken only with Moses? has he not spoken also with us? And Jehovah heard it. Now the man Moses was very meek, above all the men that were upon the face of the earth." (Num 12.1–3 ASV)

Notice that Moses' meekness is emphasized at a time when others were trying to usurp his position and he didn't respond. His only concern was God's glory, not his own, and God defended Moses' position.

So, what can we conclude about meekness from these passages? (Only a few of the passages are included. There are several more, and two of the points made are based on those not quoted.* Look them up.)

- The meek seek God and wait for God.
- The meek keep God's ordinances.
- The meek delight in peace.*
- The meek joy in the Lord.
- The meek are often of humble estate.*
- The meek are unconcerned with personal status.

God's people are meek. (If one is not meek, does that raise questions about his relationship with God?)

Hmmm… seek and wait for God, keep His ordinances, joy in Him, and are not concerned with personal status. Sounds like a meek person is one whose first thought is always 'what does God want me to do?' and/or 'will this be to God's glory?' The meek person does not consider his own desires. He is not looking for credit or acclaim. His focus is on God.

I began looking into the NT passages about meekness with the idea that the NT writers were inculcated with the OT concept of meekness, being Jews all and fluent in the OT (Luke, the lone Greek writer of the NT, never mentions meekness). Also, the same Holy Spirit guided the hands of both Old and New Testament writers. They must have used the closest Greek word available to get across the concept of meekness that God had been defining for 1500 years. That led me to disregard any study of the etymology of the four Greek words used and to understand any ambiguities by referring to the OT definition of meekness. And that led me to dumping any possibility of translating those words as gentleness. With one possible exception (1 Cor 4.21). So, let's examine some scriptures.

> Whose adorning let it not be the outward adorning of braiding the hair, and of wearing jewels of gold, or of putting on apparel; but let it be the hidden man of the heart, in the incorruptible apparel of a meek and quiet spirit, which is in the sight of God of great price. (1 Pet 3.3–4 ASV)

The meek do not care about the outward adorning of their bodies but the incorruptible apparel of meekness. They are not worried about showing personal status or garnering attention to themselves.

> Now I Paul myself entreat you by the meekness and gentleness of Christ, I who in your presence am lowly among

you, but being absent am of good courage toward you. (2 Cor 10.1 ASV)

Paul's usage shows that meekness and gentleness are distinct traits.

> I therefore, the prisoner in the Lord, beseech you to walk worthily of the calling wherewith you were called, with all lowliness and meekness. (Eph 4.1–2a ASV)

Though meekness and lowliness are similar, they express two separate responses to others based on our relationship with God.

> Put on therefore, as God's elect, holy and beloved, a heart of compassion, kindness, lowliness, meekness, longsuffering; forbearing one another, and forgiving each other, if any man has a complaint against any; even as the Lord forgave you, so also do you: and above all these things put on love, which is the bond of perfectness. And let the peace of Christ rule in your hearts, to the which also you were called in one body; and be thankful. (Col 3.12–15 ASV)

Growing in meekness is part of being God's elect with the goal being to increase in unity.

> Who is wise and understanding among you? let him show by his good life his works in meekness of wisdom. But if you have bitter jealousy and faction in your heart, glory not and lie not against the truth. (Jas 3.13–14 ASV)

A lack of meekness leads to bitter jealousy and faction because these are expressions of self rather than consideration of God.

> Brethren, if a man be overtaken in a fault, you which are spiritual, restore such an one in the spirit of meekness; considering yourself, lest you also be tempted. (Gal 6.1 KJV)

Most modern translations put "gentleness" in here, but we've already rejected that possibility, and it doesn't really make sense in the context. How would a spirit of gentleness keep me from being tempted? What temptation am I guarding against? And correcting brethren often takes more than the gentle touch to get results. Paul tells Timothy to reprove, rebuke, and exhort. Those are all powerful action words. How does one rebuke gently? Before making any conclusions, we must consider two other passages which discuss teaching the word to non-believers/erring brothers with meekness:

> …in meekness correcting them that oppose themselves; if perhaps God may give them repentance unto the knowledge of the truth. (2 Tim 2.25 ASV)

> …but sanctify in your hearts Christ as Lord: being ready always to give answer to every man that asks you a reason concerning the hope that is in you, yet with meekness and fear. (1 Pet 3.15 ASV)

Gentleness might make sense in 2 Timothy, but it doesn't really fit well in Peter's passage. If we remember that the meek person of the Old Testament is not concerned with his own status, but defers all glory to God, these passages come into better focus. When I restore an erring brother, I don't act as if I came up with all the answers myself, but in meekness I acknowledge God's scriptures and avoid the sin of arrogance and blasphemy.

When correcting those that oppose themselves, I don't act as if my own wisdom discovered the answers, but in meekness give the glory to God. In meekness, I give the reason for my hope, not that I did anything, but that God did it. In meekness, I don't concern myself with my status, but glorify God. Just like Moses. There's even a NT passage which defines this attitude:

> What do you have that you did not receive? If then you received it, why do you boast as if you did not receive it? (1 Cor 4.7)

All we have, from earthly possessions to salvation through the Gospel, we received from God. We can't act otherwise and be meek.

Conclusions about the use of meekness in the NT:

- The meek are not showy.
- Meekness leads to unity.
- Meekness involves an awareness that God gives us everything.
- Meekness buries self-interest for God's interest.

Combining what we've learned from the Old and New Testament passages, the meek seek God and seek to glorify God. The meek joy in the Lord and delight in peace, working towards unity among God's people. The meek give credit to God and are not self-promoters. Constantly being self-aware (2 Cor. 13:5) and constantly reminding ourselves of these attributes of meekness are the only real ways to overcome our natural self-concern and become meek. We must constantly remind ourselves of the awesome nature of God. One cannot, I believe, come to truly know God through the revelation of Himself in His word without instant meekness. At least in that moment. It is our duty to take that moment and extend it throughout our life-times.

16

Wisdom

It should not be the least bit surprising as we study what the Bible teaches about Christian self-improvement that Jesus is the perfect example. These last two chapters of the book will examine the life of Christ as He epitomized self-improvement.

> And Jesus increased in wisdom and in stature and in favor with God and man. (Luke 2.52)

And so we see that Jesus did, indeed, grow in several areas throughout His youth. I cannot do anything about my stature, so there is no way to emulate the Lord in that area of growth. If we are working on all the other characteristics mentioned in this book, then we will be growing in "favor with God and man". So, the one new thing mentioned here is that He grew in wisdom.

That the Son of God was able to/needed to grow in wisdom shows the incredible nature of the Lord's sacrifice. *God* had to increase in wisdom?! Job 28.20-28, along with many other passages, teaches us that God is the definition and source of all wisdom. How often, throughout Psalms and Proverbs, do we read that learning about

God and His word is the means to wisdom? And Jesus, the Son of God, the Creator of all things (John 1.3), the Upholder, Intercessor, and Possessor of the Name (Heb 1.4) had to grow in wisdom? The next time that you consider what Paul meant when he wrote to the Philippians that Jesus "emptied Himself" (2.7) when He came to live on this earth, remember that He, the source of all wisdom, had to grow in wisdom. Maybe, if we spend enough time pondering that we will catch just a glimmer of what He gave up just to begin His work of saving us.

Jesus as a young man made every effort to grow in His wisdom. As His disciples who follow His example (1 Pet 2.21), we should work to increase in wisdom as well. How? Anytime people discuss wisdom, James 1.5 comes up, and rightly so: "If any of you lacks wisdom, let him ask God, who gives generously to all without reproach, and it will be given him." As already mentioned, God is the source of all wisdom and so prayer to Him for our lack certainly makes sense, but do we pray and then sit back and wait for God to miraculously download wisdom into our brains? I'm reminded of a joke that I heard years ago:

> Floodwaters inundated Mississippi river from heavy rains well upstream. Rising waters forced one man into the second floor of his house. A neighbor came by in his fishing boat and offered to take the man to safety. "No, I don't need to be saved," the man said, "I've prayed to God for safety and I believe firmly in the power of prayer." So the neighbor went on and used his boat to save others. An hour later the flood had forced the man up onto his roof and another boat came by carrying refugees, offering to take him away

as well. Again, the man refused, citing his faith in God. Another hour passed and the man was now standing on his chimney with the water up to his chest. A National Guard helicopter flew over and let down a rope ladder to carry the man to dry land. Again, the man refused to be saved because of his faith. Shortly thereafter the man drowned. Upon reaching Heaven, the man of faith immediately marched up to God and demanded to know what had happened. "I prayed for safety and believed in you with all my heart! Why did you let me drown?" God replied, "I sent two boats and a helicopter, what more do you want?"

I think sometimes this is our attitude to growth in wisdom based on a misunderstanding of James 1:5. Yes, if we pray, He will increase our wisdom, but the only person in history who got wisdom miraculously dumped into his brain was Solomon. Maybe, instead of looking for a miracle, we should be looking for the boats and helicopters God is sending us.

How did Jesus grow in wisdom as a youth? Consider Luke's account of a scene from his childhood: "After three days they found him in the temple, sitting among the teachers, listening to them and asking them questions. And all who heard him were amazed at his understanding and his answers" (Luke 2.46–47). Jesus took every available chance to study under those who had more wisdom than he *currently* had. He listened. He asked questions. He learned. This calls to mind two passages in Proverbs: "for by wise guidance you can wage your war, and in abundance of counselors there is victory" (24.6). and "Where there is no guidance, a people falls, but in an abundance of counselors there is safety" (11.14). To grow in wisdom—in any endeavor—we need to find people wise in that area and learn from them. Ask questions. Listen to the answers. If I want to start a business, I should find successful business people and learn all I can from them. If I want to lose weight, I should talk to doctors, dieticians, and those who have already lost weight and kept it off. To know how to raise Christian children I should seek out advice from those who have successfully done so. To overcome a particularly tricky sin? I should talk with older Christians who have learned to successfully keep themselves in check. And so on. The first thing we can learn from Jesus' example of growing in wisdom is to seek out counselors in everything we do and learn from them.

Jesus also grew in wisdom because He knew His scriptures and spent time thinking about them. Remember all His discussions with the Pharisees or Sadducees when they sought to trip Him up? He almost always answered their questions with a scripture (Matt 12.3ff; 15.1ff; 19.3ff; 22.23ff; etc.). He used those passages in such a way as to show deep understanding, not just the surface meanings, but the implications of the passages. He did so without a handy-dandy bound Bible in His pocket. Jesus *knew* the scriptures. And, of course, how did Jesus defeat the three temptations of Satan in Matthew 4? By answering each with a scripture, and by knowing the scriptures well enough not to be thrown when Satan included a misused scripture in one of his temptations. And again, Jesus may well have learned the attitude toward the scriptures from the scriptures themselves:

"The law of the LORD is perfect, reviving the soul; the testimony of the LORD is sure, making wise the simple; the precepts of the LORD are right, rejoicing the heart; the commandment of the LORD is pure, enlightening the eyes; the fear of the LORD is clean, enduring forever; the rules of the LORD are true, and righteous altogether. More to be desired are they than gold, even much fine gold; sweeter also than honey and drippings of the honeycomb. Moreover, by them is your servant warned; in keeping them there is great reward." (Ps 19.7–11)

"I have more understanding than all my teachers, for your testimonies are my meditation." (Ps 119:99)

These passages alone make it clear that knowledge of the Word of God is not reserved for academics. Anyone who wishes to know the Word can simply by reading it and spending time mulling over what they read. In twelve passages the psalmist declares that he meditates on God, on God's actions and on God's word. Jesus, as a youth, followed that example and became the epitome of wisdom as a man. Maybe a similar course of action will work for me, too? If we lack wisdom it is only because we are not taking advantage of all the boats and helicopters God has made available to us.

17

Humility

Paul begins what we call the second chapter of Philippians by urging them to unity and humility:

> …complete my joy by being of the same mind, having the same love, being in full accord and of one mind. Do nothing from selfish ambition or conceit, but in humility count others more significant than yourselves. Let each of you look not only to his own interests, but also to the interests of others. (Phil 2.2–4)

Being of the same mind does not mean that we all agree on every detail of every issue, but that we agree on the doctrine of Christ and that we agree to pull together. If you have two mules in harness and one wants to walk to the left and the other to the right, we will never get anywhere, will we? We can accomplish this unity of mind if we rid ourselves of selfishness, ambition and conceit and each of us count the others as more important than ourselves. We can then give up those petty differences and pull together. Paul adds that we should, each of us, pay attention to the interests of others rather than focusing on our interests. Paul then cites Jesus as the perfect example of this.

> Have this mind among yourselves, which is yours in Christ Jesus, who, though he was in the form of God, did not count equality with God a thing to be grasped, but emptied himself, by taking the form of a servant, being born in the likeness of men. And being found in human form, he humbled himself by becoming obedient to the point of death, even death on a cross. (Phil 2.5–8)

Jesus was God. He decided not to hang on to that, but rather to give it up. Could He have refused this mission? Sure. He was God. He would have been well within His rights to decide that we were not worth the trouble, but He looked to the needs of others and counted the needs of those others (us) as being more important that Himself. Paul encourages the Philippians to live up to that example. Jesus wasn't finished teaching us, though. After He emptied Himself, He "humbled Himself by becoming obedient to the point of death". Could Jesus have lived a life of leisure? Sure. That was essentially Satan's temptation in Matthew 4. But He hadn't merely emptied Himself and become a man, Jesus humbled Himself to being obedient. Again, a mind-blowing concept: God being obedient. Gods are the bosses. In fact Baal, the name of the Canaanite deity, is simply the Canaanite word for "boss". In the Old Testament, God is known as God Almighty and God Most High. He is the Creator, and therefore owner, of all. He doesn't obey! And yet such was the extent of Christ's learned humility that He learned obedience as well (Heb 5.8).

Even in His obedience, could Christ have ended things before His death? Yes. "Do you think that I cannot appeal to my Father, and he will at once send me more than twelve legions of angels?" (Matt 26.53). The Father had provided an out. If Jesus had decided it was not worth it, He could have left. He had rights, and yet He chose to put the needs of others in front of the application of His own rights.

Throughout the New Testament, we are told that we should put our brothers' needs ahead of our own. In 1 Corinthians 6.7 Paul told the Corinthian Christians that in order to keep the church unified they should be willing to accept poor treatment. Again, he tells them that they should be willing to give up innocent pleasures if it helps their brethren (8.13). He tells the Ephesians to subject themselves to one another. In fact, the famous passage about wives being in submission to their husbands is a subset of Paul's teaching that we should all be in submission to each other. Jesus teaches His apostles in John 13 that we should all be willing to serve one another in whatever way might be necessary. Jesus, in emptying Himself, being humble, becoming obedient, and putting our needs above His rights, is the perfect example.

As Americans and as Christians, we do have rights. That is even acknowledged in Philippians 2.4 "each his own interests." We do each of us have our own things that we like and need. They are ours. We have rights! yet as a Christian my rights should be the last thing I consider. My thought process should be more along these lines:

1) In meekness, what does God want and how can I glorify Him?

2) In subjection to my brethren, what have *we* decided about dealing with this issue?

3) In love of the brethren, is there anyone who needs my help?

4) In love of the brethren, will this action harm any of my brethren?

5) In devotion to a unified body of Christ, will doing this cause disruption?

After we answer these questions, maybe we can worry about our rights.

How do we learn to be more humble? How can we be anything but when we think of the Creator emptying Himself and humiliating Himself to obedience? If our God, Savior, Creator and King can do that for us, how is it possible for me to be arrogant?

Conclusion

Christianity demands constant self-analysis and growth. This is rarely fun and never easy. We cannot coast through life and be pleasing to God. The New Testament writers unite in calling for continued, earnest effort to grow in a variety of areas.

The good news is there is a snowball effect. The more we grow in each area, the easier the others become to acquire. Growth in knowledge buttresses our faith and leads to godliness and meekness. Greater godliness and meekness makes self-control and patience more natural. Knowledge and faith brighten our joy and deepens our peace. And so on.

This is a life-long task. There is always room for improvement. Remember Paul both praising the Thessalonians' love and urging them to continued growth? We must guard against smugness: "Therefore let any who thinks that he stands, take heed lest he fall" (1 Cor 10.12). To think that we have arrived is to set ourselves up for failure. Even Paul declares that he daily disciplines himself lest he be rejected (1 Cor 9.27). If Paul exercised such caution, what care should we take?

This is work. It is hard work, continual, and lifelong. There are rewards, however. Joy and peace in this life and for eternity. Hope ensured. Having begun in 2 Peter, I leave you there also:

> For if these things are yours and abound, they make you to be not idle nor unfruitful unto the knowledge of our Lord Jesus Christ. For he that lacks these things is blind, seeing only what is near, having forgotten the cleansing from his old sins. Therefore, brethren, give the more diligence to make your calling and election sure: for if you do these things, you shall never stumble: for thus shall be richly supplied unto you the entrance into the eternal kingdom of our Lord and Savior Jesus Christ. (2 Pet 1.8–11)

For a full listing of our books, visit DeWard's website:
www.deward.com

Printed in the USA
CPSIA information can be obtained
at www.ICGtesting.com
CBHW030934120724
11387CB00016B/554